# Economic Opportunities for Women in the East Asia and Pacific Region

# Economic Opportunities for Women in the East Asia and Pacific Region

Amanda Ellis, Daniel Kirkwood, and Dhruv Malhotra

**THE WORLD BANK**
Washington, D.C.

# Contents

**Boxes**

**Figures**

## Tables

# Foreword

East Asia and the Pacific is a region of dynamic growth. Women have contributed significantly to this growth and have benefited from it through active participation in the labor market. However, women are still disproportionately represented in the informal sector and in low paid work. Efforts to identify barriers to women's business and entrepreneurial activities in the region are critical not only to facilitate inclusive growth in a national context but also to counter the increasing trend of female migratory flows in the region.

Highlighting both the challenges and the economic opportunities for businesswomen in the region offers some useful potential pointers for reform.

James Adams
Vice President
East Asia and the Pacific
World Bank

# Acknowledgments

*Economic Opportunities for Women in the East Asia and Pacific Region* was prepared by a team led by Amanda Ellis and comprising Daniel Kirkwood and Dhruv Malhotra. Nina Bhatt, Beth Delaney, Mary Hallward-Driemeier, Maria Beatriz Orlando, and Cindy Wiryakusuma provided valuable comments and suggestions as peer reviewers. Gillian Brown, Gabriela Byrde, Roger Coma-Cunill, Simeon Djankov, Alfons Eiligmann, Marie-Claude Frauenrath, Stephane Guimbert, Meg Jones, Prince Pheanuroth Sisowath, and Hans Shrader provided helpful advice on the gender dimensions of the legal and regulatory framework in the countries reviewed.

For more information on the World Bank's work on gender, visit www.worldbank.org/gender.

# Abbreviations

| | |
|---|---|
| ACE | Action Community for Entrepreneurship (Singapore) |
| ADB | Asian Development Bank |
| APEC | Asia-Pacific Economic Cooperation |
| ASEAN | Association of Southeast Asian Nations |
| CEDAW | Convention on the Elimination of All Forms of Discrimination Against Women |
| EIU | Economist Intelligence Unit (of *The Economist*) |
| EOCFW | Employer of Choice for Women (Australia) |
| EOWA | Equal Opportunity for Women in the Workplace Agency (Australia) |
| EPZ | export processing zone |
| GDP | gross domestic product |
| GNI | gross national income |
| HREOC | Human Rights and Equal Opportunity Commission (Australia) |
| ICA | investment climate assessment |
| IFC | International Finance Corporation |
| ILO | International Labour Organization |
| ITC | International Trade Centre |

| | |
|---|---|
| LDC | least developed country |
| LTC | Land Tenure Certificate |
| OECD | Organisation for Economic Co-operation and Development |
| SME | small and medium enterprise |
| SOE | state-owned enterprise |
| UNESCAP | United Nations Economic and Social Commission for Asia and the Pacific |
| WTO | World Trade Organization |

**CHAPTER 1**

# Overview

A considerable body of international evidence now suggests that gender equality matters for economic growth and that gender *in*equality can exact substantial costs in terms of lost growth (Dollar and Gatti 1999; Forbes 2000; Klasen 2002; Yamarik and Ghosh 2003; Klasen and Lamanna 2008; Ellis, Manuel, and Blackden 2006; Ellis and others 2007a, 2007b). Greater gender equality is correlated not only with higher growth outcomes, but also with lower poverty rates (Morrison, Raju, and Sinha 2007), as figure 1.1 shows.

The gender-growth nexus is increasingly being recognized by the private sector, too, both in terms of its own operations and as a macroeconomic relationship. According to analysis by global investment bank Goldman Sachs, closing the employment gender gap in the BRIC countries (Brazil, the Russian Federation, India, and China) and in the "next-11," or N-11, countries (the Arab Republic of Egypt, Bangladesh, Indonesia, the Islamic Republic of Iran, Mexico, Nigeria, Pakistan, the Philippines, the Republic of Korea, Turkey, and Vietnam) could push per capita incomes 14 percent higher than current projections by 2020 and 20 percent higher by 2030 (Lawson 2008). As Goldman Sachs chief executive Lloyd Blankfein stated, "We are disciplined in our investments, and when you get to the topic of trying to invest and create GDP, there is no better or more

**Figure 1.1    Poverty Headcount vs. Relative Female Human Development, 1997**

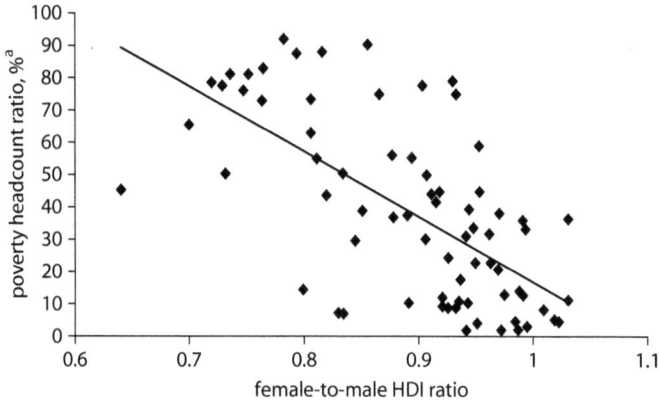

Source: Morrison, Raju, and Sinha 2007.
Note: Scatter plot for 73 developing countries. Poverty headcount ratio statistics are based on the international poverty line of $2.16 per day (1993 PPP $) and are obtained from the World Bank's World Development Indicators database.
Male and female HDIs for 1997 were calculated using data from the 1999 HDR statistical database. See Klasen 2006 for
the formula to obtain the gender-specific HDIs. When the poverty headcount ratio statistic for a given country is
unavailable for 1997, the closest year to 1997 with available data (in the 1998–2003 period) is used. $R^2 = 0.4287$;
HDI = Human Development Index; PPP = purchasing power parity; HDR = Human Development Report.
a. The poverty headcount ratio (percentage of population below the national poverty line) is the proportion
of the national population whose incomes fall below the offical threshold set by the government.

efficient investment—no lower hanging fruit in the world to pick—than
the investment you make in women."

There is a theoretically plausible link between gender equality and
growth. To underuse the human capital of half the population arguably
reduces national growth potential. This is especially true where barriers
unrelated to inherent productivity displace more-productive female
workers from the labor force in favor of relatively less-productive male
workers. Conversely, where more women can play a role in the formal
labor market, national production levels and earnings increase, and there
are more workers to contribute to economic growth and poverty reduction (Buvinic and King 2007). Indeed, both Young (1995) and Krugman
(1994) attribute much of East Asia's rapid economic growth to factor
accumulation (both physical and human capital), which includes the
increase in female labor force participation. Additionally, economically
active women are more likely to have greater control of family resources,
and evidence shows that women are more likely than men to invest
more resources in their children's health and education, thus passing the
benefits on to future generations (Buvinic and King 2007).

Comparing the development successes of the East Asia and Pacific region[1] with other developing regions makes the argument linking gender equality and economic growth compelling. East Asia and the Pacific has been the fastest growing, economically, of all developing regions; between 1960 and 2000, real per capita growth was 4.05 percent, compared with 0.57 percent in Sub-Saharan Africa and 2.24 percent in the Middle East and North Africa (Klasen and Lamanna 2008).

At the same time, many East Asian and Pacific countries have made substantial inroads toward reducing poverty and unemployment as they have built on their human capital (including girls and women). Today, the region boasts one of the narrowest gender gaps in terms of economic participation (ILO 2008). Recent cross-country regression analysis of data spanning a 40-year period (1960–2000) suggests that greater gender equality explains a substantial portion of the superior growth in the East Asia and the Pacific region[2] relative to the South Asia and the Middle East and North Africa regions (Klasen and Lamanna 2008).[3] This relative gap in economic performance is likely to widen, and the relative growth costs are likely to increase, because the gender gaps in employment are shrinking much faster in the East Asia and Pacific region than in either the Middle East and North Africa or the South Asia regions (Klasen and Lamanna 2008).[4]

This gender-growth nexus is directly relevant to the subject of this publication: creating economic opportunities for women by leveling the playing field through equitable rules for women and men. Research suggests that the ease of doing business (one aspect of the rules) correlates with higher shares of female entrepreneurs and women in the labor force (World Bank 2007). Figure 1.2 shows this correlation, grouping countries into quintiles according to the ease of doing business on the horizontal axes and the percentages of female entrepreneurs (as a percentage of all entrepreneurs) and female unemployment (as a proportion of men's) on the vertical axes.

Furthermore, there is a positive correlation between outcomes for women as entrepreneurs and outcomes for women in wage-earning and salaried work. The scatter plots in figure 1.3 show global correlations between the female-male ratios of employers and the female-male ratios of wage-earning and salaried workers. Even controlling for gross domestic product (GDP) per capita, the correlation is positive. The same factors that drive increased entrepreneurship and firm ownership presumably drive participation in secure paid employment. The expansion of women's opportunities to lead viable enterprises on an equal footing with men goes

**Figure 1.2    Correlations between Ease of Doing Business and Women's Economic Participation**

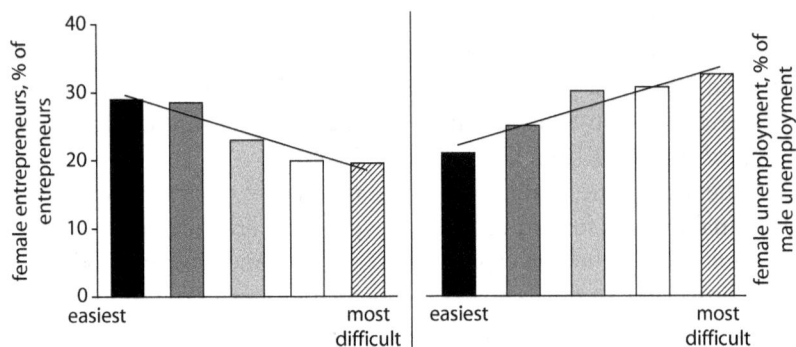

Source: World Bank 2007.
Note: Countries arranged by Ease of Doing Business ranking quintile. Relationships are significant at the 1 percent level and remain significant when controlling for income per capita.

hand in hand with their increased participation in secure and decent work. "By teaching and encouraging women to become their own bosses, we contribute to solutions to poverty and unemployment," says Myrna Yao, chair of the National Commission on the Role of Filipino Women (World Bank 2010).

From this point of view, a level playing field for women-led businesses is an essential policy focus for governments wanting to realize equal economic opportunities for women and reap the associated benefits. This report takes no position on whether women *should* participate as entrepreneurs (though the potential benefits are discussed) but rather analyzes whether gender-related barriers prevent the women who want or need to participate from doing so.

## Regional Performance

Impressive regional gains in gender equity notwithstanding, women continue to face barriers in realizing their entrepreneurial potential in East Asian and the Pacific economies. The region has done considerably better *relative* to other developing regions by narrowing gaps in many economic dimensions—specifically labor market participation and development of human capital through sustained investment in both girls' and boys' education. But in *absolute* terms, gaps persist. For example, the gender gap in labor force participation is present in all regions, including the East Asia

**Figure 1.3    Global Correlation between Female Entrepreneurship and Employment, Selected East Asian and Pacific Economies Highlighted**

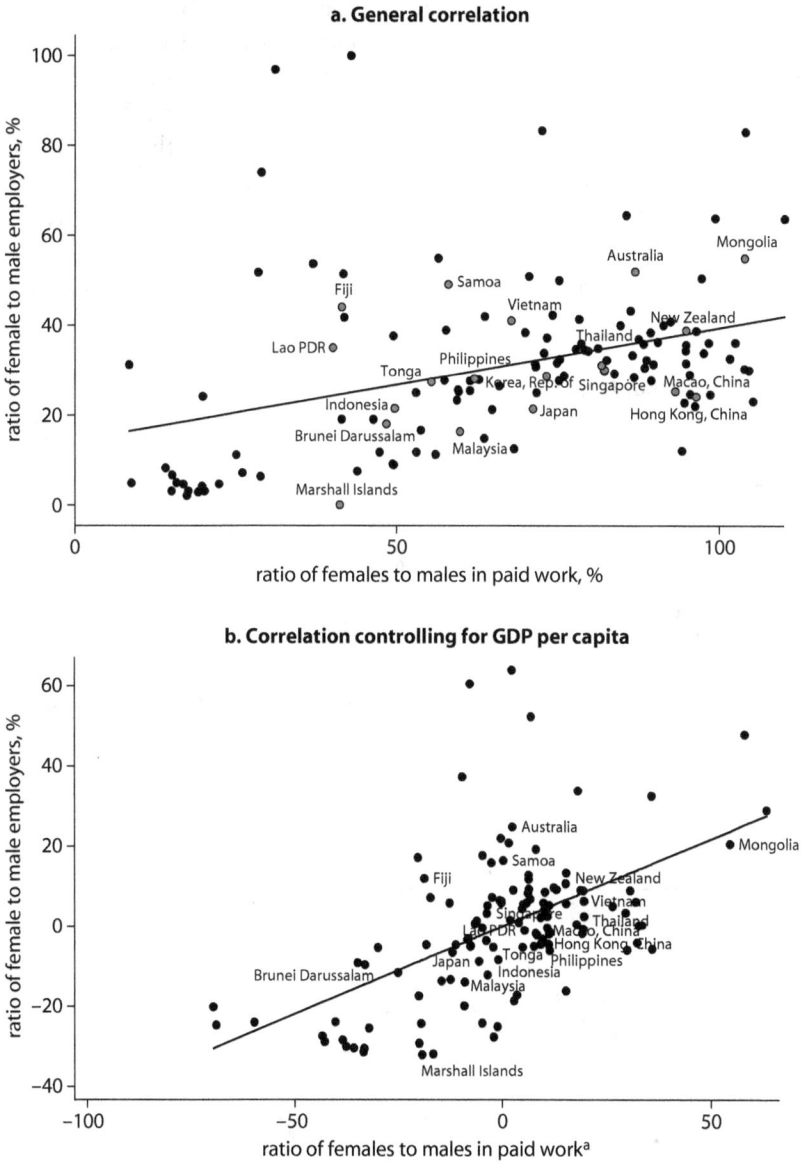

**a. General correlation**

**b. Correlation controlling for GDP per capita**

*Source:* International Labour Organization Key Indicators of the Labour Market database, latest available data, 1981–2008.
*Note:* GDP = gross domestic product.
a. coef = .43686032, se = .06175286, t = 7.07.

and Pacific and high-income regions. Indeed, a paper by the United Nations Economic and Social Commission for Asia and the Pacific (UNESCAP) finds that the region is "losing $42–47 billion per year because of restrictions on women's access to employment opportunities—and another $16–30 billion per year because of gender gaps in education" (UNESCAP 2007). However, the gap is much smaller in the East Asia and Pacific region than in other developing regions; compare, for example, the median East Asia and Pacific country with the median country in the Sub-Saharan Africa, South Asia, or Middle East and North Africa regions (figure 1.4).

Some inequalities, such as lower mandatory retirement ages for women, are driven by gender differentiation in laws and statutes, but such

**Figure 1.4    Labor Force Participation, by Sex**

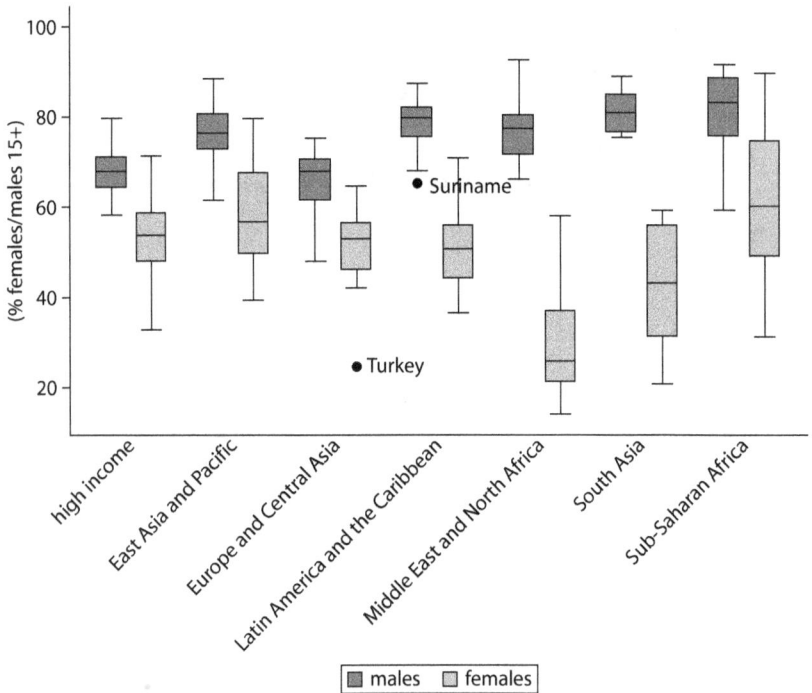

Source: International Labour Organization.
Note: Boxes show 25th to 75th percentiles. Bars within the boxes show the median value. End bars show the upper and lower adjacent values. Regions are defined according to World Bank Group Classification.
"High income" designates all those countries (regardless of geography, except if they are in the Middle East) whose gross national income per capita (Atlas Method) in 2008 was greater than US$11,906. For definition of geographic and high-income regions, see note to figure 2.7.

discrimination is much less prevalent than in other regions, such as the Middle East and North Africa or Sub-Saharan Africa. More often, in the more conservative societies of East Asia and the Pacific, implicit biases, customs, and traditions constrain women's economic opportunities, as the qualitative case studies of individual female entrepreneurs in this publication will illustrate. For example, early marriage can often be a proxy for wider attitudes toward females in the household and can constrain their economic opportunities even where laws and customs are equal for men and women. Figure 1.5 depicts the correlation between the proportion of women who marry early and the ratio of females to males in wage-earning and salaried work. The negative correlation is striking and remains significant even when controlling for GDP per capita.

Additionally, although aggregate or regional changes look decidedly positive, the averages can hide significant intraregional and intracountry disparities. In particular, female entrepreneurs continue to face a variety of constraints. Figure 1.6 shows the gender gap in entrepreneurship for several countries in the East Asia and Pacific region. The fight for equal economic opportunity for women is thus not over, even in this well-performing region, and more must be done to simplify the business environment for, and change attitudes toward, women entrepreneurs.

## Framework for Analysis

While gaps between men's and women's levels of entrepreneurship exist in all the East Asia and Pacific countries, they vary in dimension and scope. This variance should be expected because of the region's considerable socioeconomic diversity. Its countries represent the full spectrum of income levels—from least developed countries (LDCs) such as Lao PDR and the Solomon Islands to high-income "Asian tigers" such as Hong Kong, China, and Singapore. They range from sparsely populated Pacific islands to the most populous country, China, with 1.3 billion inhabitants. Primarily agrarian economies such as Lao PDR coexist with mixed economies, such as China and Thailand, as well as industrial and tertiary-sector-dominated economies such as Australia, New Zealand, and Singapore. Finally, regulatory regimes vary—from laissez-faire Hong Kong, China and Singapore—to the socialist-oriented market economies of Lao PDR and Vietnam.

This socioeconomic diversity, in turn, affects the types of constraints that women entrepreneurs face in starting, operating, and growing their businesses. Therefore, a country-specific analysis of these barriers must supplement the regional analysis.

**Figure 1.5    Global Correlation of Early Marriage and Female/Male Paid Worker Ratio, Selected East Asian and Pacific Economies Highlighted**

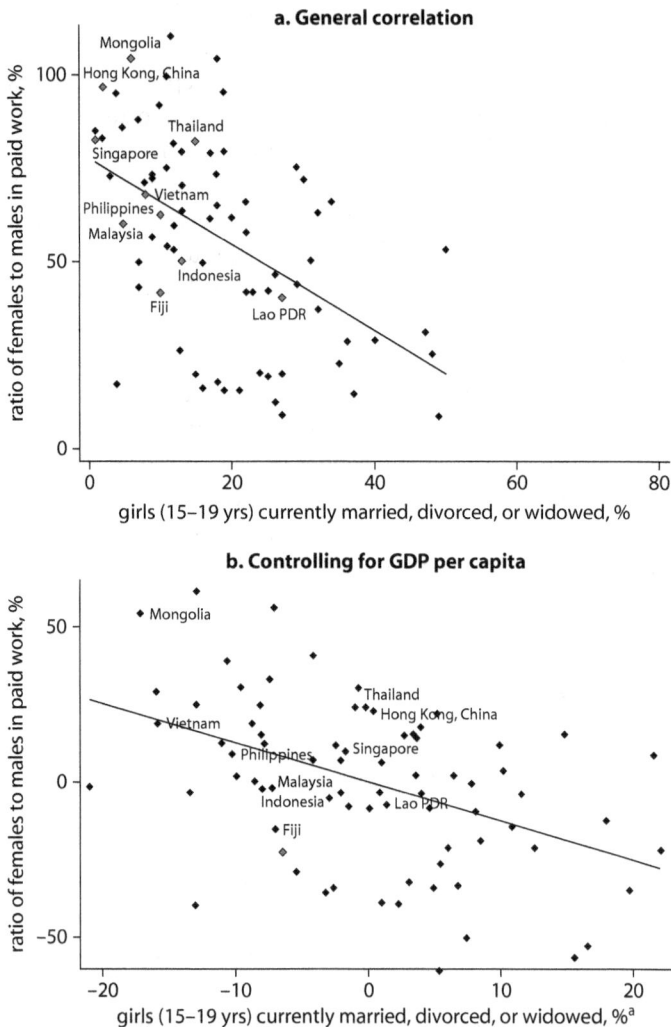

**a. General correlation**

ratio of females to males in paid work, %

Mongolia
Hong Kong, China
Thailand
Singapore
Vietnam
Philippines
Malaysia
Indonesia
Fiji
Lao PDR

girls (15–19 yrs) currently married, divorced, or widowed, %

**b. Controlling for GDP per capita**

ratio of females to males in paid work, %

Mongolia
Thailand
Hong Kong, China
Vietnam
Singapore
Philippines
Malaysia
Indonesia
Lao PDR
Fiji

girls (15–19 yrs) currently married, divorced, or widowed, %[a]

*Source:* International Labour Organization Key Indicators of the Labour Market database, latest available data, 1981–2008.
*Note:* GDP = gross domestic product.
a. coef = −1.2393199, se = .27765358, t = −4.46.

Broadly speaking, the following issues, all important to women's economic opportunity, must be addressed to varying degrees throughout the region:

- *Access to assets:* The degree to which women in the region have access to land and capital on equal or unequal terms is critical to

**Figure 1.6    Proportion of Men and Women Engaged in Entrepreneurship, Formal and Informal, Selected East Asian and Pacific Economies**

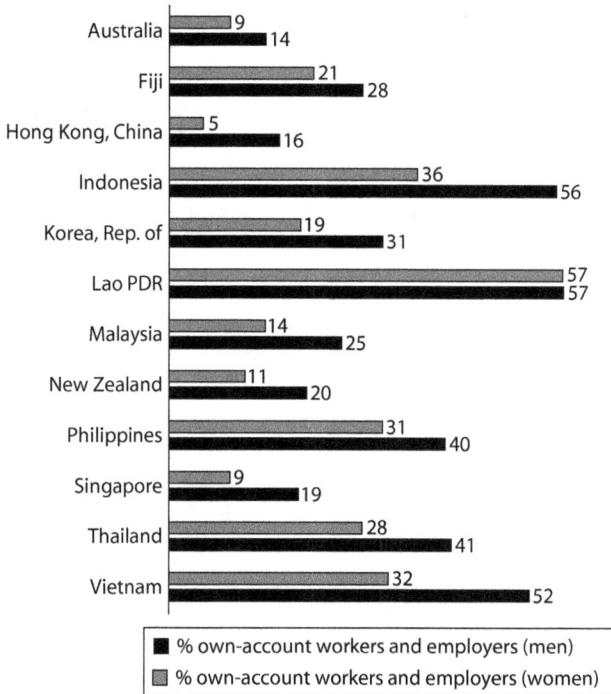

Source: International Labour Organization Key Indicators of the Labour Market, latest available data, 1998–2008.
Note: "Entrepreneurs" are the proportions of men and women classified as "employers" or "own-account workers" in the International Labour Organization Key Indicators of the Labour Market database. Employers are those workers who, working on their own account or with one or few partners, hold the type of job defined as a "self-employment job" and, in this capacity, on a continuous basis (including the reference period) have engaged one or more persons to work for them in their business as "employee(s)." Self-employment jobs are those jobs in which the remuneration depends directly upon the profits (or potential profits) derived from the goods and services produced (where own consumption is considered to be part of the profits). "Own-account" workers are those workers who, working on their own account or with one or more partners, hold a "self-employment job" and have not engaged on a continuous basis any "employees" to work for them during the reference period. The sum of these two categories captures, we believe, the proportion of the labor force that owns formal sector enterprises ("employers") and those who are in the microenterprise sector—which may or may not be formal "own-account workers."

their entrepreneurial opportunities. Access to internal assets (human capital and time) is also important and often influences access to capital.

- *Business regulations:* Cumbersome and complex legal requirements—the sheer number of them as well as the cost and time required for compliance—can present formidable obstacles. For example, high business registration costs may affect women more than men because women tend to have less time to devote to their businesses. Moreover, if women do not register their businesses, they cannot take advantage of the risk-optimizing features of limited liability; they don't have access to social safety nets for themselves and their employees; they have less access to the capital available to formally registered businesses (making it harder to expand their businesses and making them more likely to remain informal); and they cannot legally enforce contracts.

- *Governance:* The role and effectiveness of public-private dialogue and women's influence in policy formation and other governance issues, such as corruption, also affect the business environment in crucial ways.
- *Conditions for enterprise growth:* Several factors affect growth beyond the microstage or small-scale stage. These include regulations affecting the ease of cross-border trade; access to specialized business and vocational training; availability of adequate child care (given the usually unequal pressure on women's time to fulfill family responsibilities); and the presence and effectiveness of intermediary organizations.

These factors affect women-owned businesses at all stages of their existence: when the decision to go into business is first made (for which access to assets is a prerequisite); at start-up; during day-to-day operations (for which regulations and governance are of prime importance); and, finally, while growing a business (in which training, technical support, and access to larger markets all play significant roles).

The organizing framework of our analysis, which figure 1.7 illustrates, includes all of these themes. While laws, institutions, culture, and norms shape entrepreneurial processes and outcomes for women, they are, of course, only part of the story. Other determinants include broader trends in human capital accumulation and the intrahousehold allocation decisions that women make at several points in their lives. Moreover, secular changes in economic and social structures—for example, due to urbanization and fertility transitions—also play a role. While the determinants of women's economic empowerment are complex and varied, the scope of this analysis is limited to the institutional environment for business entry and operations, including the influence of domestic legislation. This focus is relevant to this publication's objective: to highlight entry points for policy change that can engender private sector development.

In analyzing the barriers to female entrepreneurship, areas of progress in the region, and problems that require further action, this work draws on the following sources:

- Quantitative data from the *Doing Business 2010* report (World Bank 2009)

**Figure 1.7    Organizing Framework for the Analysis**

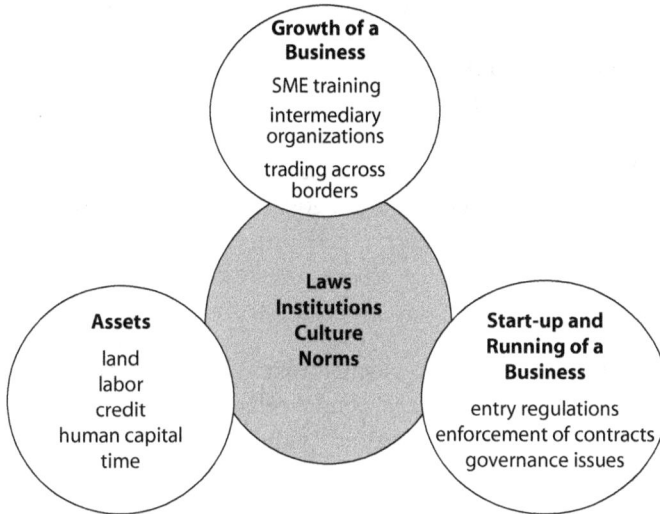

Growth of a
Business

SME training
intermediary
organizations
trading across
borders

Assets

land
labor
credit
human capital
time

Laws
Institutions
Culture
Norms

Start-up and
Running of a
Business

entry regulations
enforcement of contracts
governance issues

*Source:* Authors.

- Evidence from World Bank country-level investment climate assessments (ICAs), enterprise surveys (especially with sex-disaggregated data), and qualitative and quantitative analyses conducted through a gender lens
- Qualitative analysis (codified in scores) conducted as part of a forthcoming Economist Intelligence Unit product on women's economic opportunity (EIU forthcoming)
- Qualitative insights from World Bank case studies of individual female entrepreneurs in East Asia and the Pacific (World Bank 2010)

## Main Findings

While the East Asia and Pacific region has performed well in terms of economic growth and gender equality over the past few decades, the fight for gender equality in the economic sphere is far from won. As long as there are still significant intraregional differences and challenges to leveling the playing field for men and women, increasing economic participation in quantitative terms is not enough. Genuine equality requires that women enjoy the same *opportunities* as men—including opportunities to take entrepreneurial risks and be their own bosses, should they so wish.

On the positive side, many countries in the region have taken significant steps toward unleashing the economic potential of women:

- Reforming the legal property-rights framework to remove discriminatory provisions against women
- Improving the business environment by simplifying business entry and adopting e-government processes and "one-stop shops" where businesses can complete required government importing and exporting procedures
- Increasing opportunities for productive women-led businesses to grow above and beyond the micro and small sectors

This publication presents evidence that the region could benefit further from significant unrealized gender-related growth potential. Many reasons for this are country specific. At the regional level, however, several commonalities emerge:

- Whereas laws are mostly equal for men and women on paper (unlike countries in developing regions such as the Middle East, South Asia, or Africa), institutions may not adequately implement these laws in a gender-equal manner, because of lack of capacity, will, or both.
- Cultural attitudes and normative discrimination still prevent women and girls from participating equally with men as paid workers, as business operators and owners, and as asset holders.
- Regulations governing business start-up, operation, and growth often unduly constrain both women and men, but they may affect women more severely because women tend to have less time to deal with onerous regulations due to often-unequal family and household responsibilities.
- Women continue to receive less business training and development than men, and the proverbial glass ceiling often prevents women from getting the managerial experience that can help them succeed as entrepreneurs.
- Workplace policies—such as maternity leave provision, statutory retirement ages, and affordable child care—are often not friendly to women.

Unlocking the hidden growth potential of greater economic equality will require more than changes to government policy and practice. It will also require transformation of the subtle cultural context in which women-led businesses operate. This long-term process will change institutions, established ways of operating and doing business, and, most important, attitudes.

In the medium term, governments and economies stand to benefit by engendering private sector development policy, by ironing out remaining statutory inequalities, and by creating an enabling environment for women-led businesses. But policy cannot be formulated, sequenced, or prioritized without adequate data. One of the most pressing needs governments must address is the collection of sex-disaggregated statistics on the obstacles that female entrepreneurs face and policies that could help mitigate those obstacles. In particular, policy makers need data about the following:

- The extent to which discriminatory law and practices at the country level affect women's access to assets, particularly where the law diverges from customary practice. To develop policies that ameliorate unequal access to assets, governments need data about gender-based differences in the costs of and access to credit, time use and time poverty, and skills gaps.
- The extent to which business regulations affect women relative to men, particularly in the context of women's relative lack of access to time and social networks, which are crucial to navigating difficult bureaucratic procedures. Data are also needed on the costs of women's lack of access to information (regarding rights, credit, and so on) to formulate targeted information provision policies.
- Cost-benefit analyses of policies that could help women grow their businesses
- How government services in sectors such as infrastructure, water, and justice differ in quality and quantity for women versus men, and how these differences affect enterprise start-up and operations

Understanding which constraints are the most binding for women is crucial for the appropriate prioritization and sequencing of reforms. For example, legal and regulatory reform is unlikely to have the intended results if women are unaware of their rights or if they face prohibitive costs to secure their economic rights (to assets, to fair commercial dispute resolution, and so on). Similarly, equal access to assets (for example, land, credit, and labor) is unlikely to catalyze entrepreneurship without simplification of the legal and regulatory requirements for starting a business and (where relevant) trading across borders.

This analysis is exploratory, and further analysis of sex-disaggregated research and data on the East Asia and Pacific region's business environments and regulatory burdens would deepen our understanding of the most binding constraints on female entrepreneurs. The ultimate goal of this publication is to highlight these constraints and to suggest areas for reform that policy makers may tailor to the needs of different countries. Removing these constraints and investing in women is, to borrow from Goldman Sachs's Lloyd Blankfein, a "low-hanging fruit" in the project of creating prosperous, equal societies.

## Notes

1. We define the region according to the World Bank regional classification, which includes both developing East Asia and Australia and New Zealand. For interregional (including quantitative) comparisons on specific issues, the focus is usually on developing East Asia unless otherwise noted. However, we include case studies from the developed countries (including the United States, which is an Asia-Pacific Economic Cooperation [APEC] country but not an East Asia and Pacific country) because they present examples of regulatory good practice, public-private dialogue, and women-friendly workplace policies (such as maternity leave provisioning) that are potential blueprints for positive change.

2. Klasen and Lamanna's analysis concentrates on developing East Asia and does not include developed APEC countries such as Australia and New Zealand.

3. More specifically, the data point to the combined effect of gender gaps in education and labor force participation, as a proxy for gender gaps in employment.

4. We must acknowledge the possibility of reverse causality, which is not easily discernible by this kind of cross-country work. In particular, the question is whether greater economic opportunity for women increases growth in East Asian and Pacific economies or whether higher income levels (due to better growth performance, driven by factors *other* than women's economic equality and access to education) lead to policy reforms that, in turn, foster greater economic participation by women. Klasen and Lamanna control for this possible endogeneity (as well as for unobserved heterogeneity) in their regressions by adopting a panel data framework. Their estimations treat each decade of the 40-year period under study (1960–2000) as one observation using *initial* values of the explanatory variables. By using the beginning-of-decade values of the labor force participation and education gap variables and regressing on end-of-decade growth figures, one can expect that endogeneity will be at least partially controlled.

# References

Buvinic, M., and E. King. 2007. "Smart Economics." *Finance and Development* (International Monetary Fund) 44 (2): 6–11. http://www.imf.org/external/pubs/ft/fandd/2007/06/king.htm#author.

Dollar, D., and R. Gatti. 1999. "Gender Inequality, Income and Growth: Are Good Times Good for Women?" Working Paper 20771, World Bank, Washington, DC.

EIU (Economist Intelligence Unit). Forthcoming. "Women's Economic Opportunity Index." Draft report, EIU, London.

Ellis, A., C. Manuel, and M. Blackden. 2006. *Gender and Economic Growth in Uganda: Unleashing the Power of Women.* Directions in Development Series. Washington, DC: World Bank.

Ellis, A., M. Blackden, J. Cutura, F. MacCullock, and H. Seebems. 2007a. *Gender and Economic Growth in Tanzania: Creating Economic Opportunities for Women.* Directions in Development Series. Washington, DC: World Bank.

Ellis, A., J. Cutura, N. Dioune, I. Gillson, C. Manuel, and J. Thongori. 2007b. *Gender and Economic Growth in Kenya: Unleashing the Power of Women.* Directions in Development Series. Washington, DC: World Bank.

Forbes, K. 2000. "A Reassessment of the Relationship between Inequality and Growth." *American Economic Review* 90 (4): 869–87.

ILO (International Labour Organization). 2008. "Global Employment Trends for Women 2008: More Women Enter the Workforce, but More than Half of All Working Women Are in Vulnerable Jobs." Press Release, March 6. http://www.ilo.org/global/About_the_ILO/Media_and_public_information/Press_releases/lang--en/WCMS_091102/index.htm.

Klasen, S. 2002. "Low Schooling for Girls, Slower Growth for All?" *World Bank Economic Review* 16 (3): 345–73.

Klasen, S. 2006. "UNDP's Gender-Related Measures: Some Conceptual Problems and Possible Solutions. *Journal of Human Development* 7 (2): 244–74.

Klasen, S., and F. Lamanna. 2008. "The Impact of Gender Inequality in Education and Employment on Economic Growth in Developing Countries: Updates and Extensions." Discussion Paper 175, Ibero-America Institute for Economic Research, Göttingen, Germany. http://www2.vwl.wiso.uni-goettingen.de/ibero/papers/DB175.pdf.

Krugman, Paul. 1994. "The Myth of Asia's Miracle." *Foreign Affairs* 73 (6): 62–78.

Lawson, S. 2008. "Women Hold Up Half the Sky." Global Economics Paper 164, Goldman Sachs, New York.

Morrison, A., D. Raju, and N. Sinha. 2007. "Gender Equality, Poverty, and Economic Growth." Policy Research Working Paper 4349, World Bank, Washington, DC.

UNESCAP (United Nations Economic and Social Commission for Asia and the Pacific). 2007. *Economic and Social Survey of Asia and the Pacific 2007.* Bangkok: UNESCAP. http://www.unescap.org/survey2007.

World Bank. 2007. *Doing Business 2008.* Washington, DC: World Bank.

———. 2009. *Doing Business 2010.* Washington, DC: World Bank.

———. 2010. *"Economic Opportunities for Women in the East Asia and Pacific Region."* Washington, DC: World Bank.

Yamarik, Steven, and Sucharita Ghosh. 2003. "Is Female Education Productive? A Reassessment." Photocopy. Tufts University, Medford, MA. http://www.csulb.edu/~syamarik/Papers/FemaleEd.pdf.

Young, Alwyn. 1995. "The Tyranny of Numbers: Confronting the Statistical Realities of the East Asian Growth Experience." *The Quarterly Journal of Economics* 110 (3): 641–80.

# CHAPTER 2

# Access to Assets

Access to assets is a crucial factor to an entrepreneur's ability to start a business, and the evidence suggests that this access has a gendered dimension: Inequalities in the East Asia and Pacific region reduce the security and extent of women's access to assets relative to men's. This disparity, in turn, determines whether, and to what extent, women can realize equal economic opportunities.

Two kinds of assets are relevant to an analysis of economic opportunities, as figure 2.1 shows: (1) external assets (or factors of production) such as land, labor, and credit, and (2) internal assets of the entrepreneur herself such as vocational and business skills, freedom from time poverty, and human capital.

The extent to which women have secure and equal access to relevant assets is shaped by the influence of laws and regulations, mediated by norms, cultural values, and institutions.

## External Assets

Women's access to external assets—including land, labor, and credit—determines whether they even have the means of production to start and operate a business. Equality of access to these assets is thus fundamental to women's ability to participate and advance in economic life.

**Figure 2.1    Assets that Affect Opportunities for Entrepreneurship**

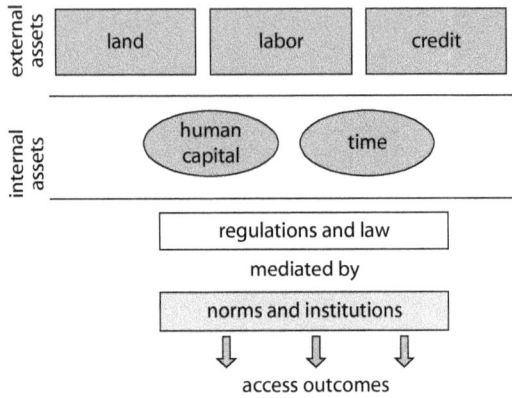

*Source:* Authors.

## Land

Secure rights to property generally, and to land in particular, are crucial to entrepreneurial agency and success in the region because collateral-based lending continues to be the dominant form of lending, especially in developing countries (OECD 2003; Sheng 2003; Gochoco-Baustista 2009). Women's access to land thus determines, in part, their access to credit, which is crucial for starting and expanding their businesses.

Where women's property rights are insecure, or not granted at all because of discriminatory inheritance and matrimonial laws and practices, women either cannot go into business or end up operating informally in small enterprises or microenterprises. In addition, where property is registered only in their husbands' names, women may be forced to take out loans and register businesses in their husbands' names, forgoing ultimate control of their businesses.

That discriminatory practices can affect economic outcomes for women is shown in figure 2.2, which plots the correlations between female-to-male adult literacy ratios and employer ratios, disaggregated by country performance on the Organisation for Economic Co-operation and Development's (OECD) Inheritance Practices Indicator. As discrimination increases, the correlation becomes progressively flatter. Again, correlation does not imply causality. What we can take away from this simple correlation, however, is that discriminatory practices can potentially distort the relationships between normal labor market outcomes and education through their interaction with women's access to assets.

**Figure 2.2     Correlations of Female-to-Male Employer and Adult Literacy Ratios by Inheritance Practices**

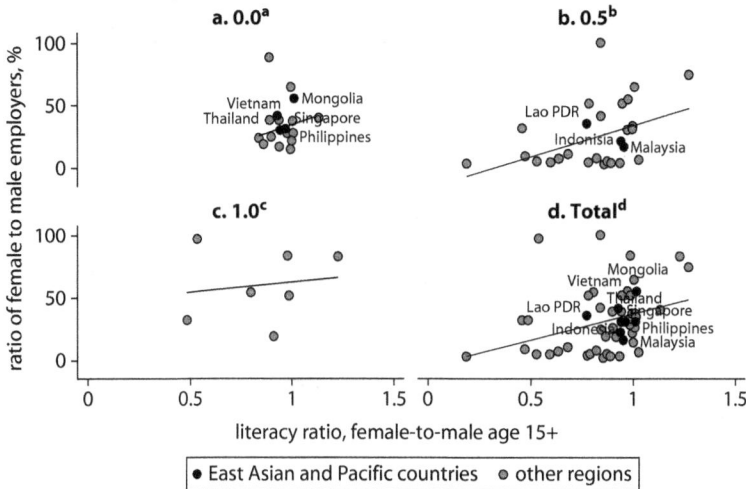

*Sources:* Organisation for Economic Co-operation and Development Inheritance Practices Indicator, Gender and Institution Database; International Labour Organization Key Indicators of the Labour market database, latest available data, 1981–2008.
*Note:* Graphs by inheritance practices in favor of male heirs (level between 0 = no and 1 = yes).

When analyzing female entrepreneurs' access to land, three kinds of rights are relevant: the right to *own* land, the right to *control* land, and the right to *transfer or trade* land. On all three dimensions, case-study and cross-country evidence (echoing findings in many other developing regions; see, for example, Agarwal 1994 on South Asia and Wanyeki 2003 on Africa) for East Asia and the Pacific suggests that two kinds of inequality constrain land rights:

- *De jure inequality* affects women where statutory and customary laws are inherently discriminatory against women. Relevant laws and regulations include those governing matrimonial assets, inheritance (including intestacy), and joint titling.
- *De facto inequality* occurs where discriminatory customs and norms override laws that are formally equal or where inadequate implementation constrains women's theoretically equal rights.

In some countries, the legal framework of property rights explicitly favors men. In others, the law is silent on gender, and so formal equality is implicit. Finally, and encouragingly, several East Asian and Pacific countries have explicit formal legal provisions guaranteeing equal property and land rights for women.

Indonesia's statutory legal framework exemplifies overt discrimination with respect to transfer rights, resulting in de jure inequality. Article 108 of the Indonesian Civil Code prevents women from entering into contracts on their own behalf, whether to sell or to buy property. This means that men can decide whether their wives have access to collateral (IFC 2006c) and whether they can raise or invest capital through the buying or selling of land. Research suggests that access to land can be precarious for women in Indonesia, with loss of control and ownership rights (in addition to lack of transfer rights) upon divorce, widowhood, male migration, or desertion by husbands (Land Tenure Center 2003).

Papua New Guinea's customary laws, which determine ownership of about 90 percent of land, similarly restrict women's access to land. Matrilineal principles govern land in some areas, but even there, brothers and male relatives are the real decision makers. Only two of the country's supposedly matrilineal societies grant women substantive equal rights in land mediation and authority to trade in their own capacity (ADB 2006c).

Elsewhere in the region, women's legal rights to land are restricted to use rights, with women unable to own or, therefore, to transfer or control land. This is the situation, for example, in Timor-Leste (ADB 2005). In Tonga, the law of succession in the Constitution of Tonga discriminates against daughters by ensuring that only the eldest son may inherit estates and titles; only if there are no living sons can daughters inherit (Pacific Islands Legal Information Institute). The threat to this legal inequality that the Convention on the Elimination of all Forms of Discrimination Against Women (CEDAW) poses has been cited as one of the main reasons that Tonga remains one of the few countries in the world yet to have signed CEDAW (New Zealand Pacific Business Council 2009).

Other countries have explicitly enshrined gender equality in land-rights law, which ensures at least de jure equality—for example, in Cambodia; China; Hong Kong, China; the Philippines, and Singapore (World Bank n.d.). As a practical matter, however, a formally equal legal framework does not always ensure equal property rights for men and women for two main reasons: (1) discriminatory customs play a strong role in some localities, and (2) inadequate implementation of gender-equal or gender-neutral land laws perpetuates, in practice, gender-related differences in property rights.

Traditional norms complicate the extent to which equal legal provisions bring equal property access for women. In some cases, traditional customs can distort or supersede national laws, regulations, or constitutional provisions guaranteeing gender equality in control, exchange, and inheritance of property. In China, for example, the Law on the Protection of Rights and Interests of Women and the Marriage Law give women equal land rights, including in situations of marriage, divorce, and inheritance (World Bank n.d.). Rural customs dictate, however, that when a woman marries a man from another village, she must move to his village and leave her land behind, thus abrogating her rights to use land in her home village (ADB 2006a).

In Cambodia, too, while the 2001 land law sets out equal land rights, women's ability to take advantage of these rights is lessened by customary views that the man is the head of the household and therefore responsible for the household's land (ADB 2004). Similarly, in the Philippines, women have the equal right to enter into contracts under the Philippines Women in Development and Nation Building Act (Act No. 7192), yet in practice women often need their husbands' consent for land-related transactions (World Bank n.d.). A case study of a female entrepreneur in the Philippines provides a telling illustration of this barrier (see box 2.1).

---

**Box 2.1**

## Case Study Excerpt

### The Philippines: Pacita Juan
Chief executive and owner, Figaro Coffee

Pacita Juan combined a taste for coffee and a nose for deals to develop a successful business model: franchising. Franchising has not only helped Juan's business become the second-largest coffee company in the Philippines, but also helped other aspiring entrepreneurs overcome problems such as lack of credit and red tape in business start-up.

Starting a business and getting access to credit can be particularly challenging for Filipino entrepreneurs. The Philippines scored 155 in the 2009 *Doing Business* Starting a Business Indicator, requiring an average of 52 days and 15 procedures (World Bank 2008). In the *Doing Business* Getting Credit Indicator, it ranked 123rd globally out of 181 countries (World Bank 2008). "Women have a lot of informal small businesses that aren't scalable because women don't have the means to take them to the next level," Juan says. Realizing that there could be a different way for her business to scale up, Juan turned to franchising her emerging brand. Figaro awarded its first franchise in 1998.

*(continued)*

**Box 2.1** *(continued)*

As a franchisor, Juan helps her franchisees get access to credit by acting as guarantor for their loans. She worked with the government to develop a special credit product for franchises and is now partnering with the Women's Business Council to persuade commercial banks to better address the needs of women in business. The franchising model has additional benefits for new aspiring businesswomen: It helps franchisees navigate the maze of procedures for setting up their businesses while also providing a proven business operation system.

"We already know what it takes to get a permit. So we do other things at the same time," Juan says. "We hire people, train them, do the signage, check out the plans. . . . Because of our experience we know how many days it takes in each city. And, of course, the officials know the brand already."

Figaro Coffee now has close to 80 outlets—more than half of which are franchises—with a total annual turnover of $10 million–$15 million and a workforce of 600 to 700.

*Source:* World Bank 2008.

In Indonesia, the laws governing matrimonial property worsen the already disadvantaged position of women regarding land ownership, as discussed above. Although the 1975 Marriage Law provides for joint ownership of property acquired during marriage, the marital property is usually registered only in the husband's name.

Even seemingly gender-neutral systems, where the law is silent on gender, may be inadequate in combating gender inequalities, sometimes because of faulty implementation. In Vietnam in the 1990s, for example, land law did not explicitly discriminate against women, but the required Land Tenure Certificates (LTCs) provided space for just one name. Because men were usually the ones who registered land, the LTCs usually listed only their names. Consequently, without legal proof of their land rights, women could not use the land, for example, as collateral for loans. Where property is registered only in their husbands' names, women's only option for getting business loans may be to take out loans and register businesses in their husbands' names, thus forgoing ultimate control of their businesses. The World Bank worked with the government of Vietnam to implement Decree 70 (effective in 2001), which requires that all family assets and land-use rights be registered in the name of both husband and wife. The project provided new LTCs with space for two names: both husband and wife. However, it was not just the technical task of fixing the

LTCs that was important; improving both men's and women's knowledge of land rights was another crucial element of the project. Village meetings, leaflets, and messages broadcast on loudspeakers were all used to spread the word (World Bank 2002).

As long as female entrepreneurs or government officials who implement the laws remain unaware of women's legal rights, those rights are rendered less effective. Concerns about this lack of awareness have arisen in Cambodia, Indonesia, Lao PDR, and Vietnam. In Lao PDR, such concerns motivated the World Bank and the Australian Agency for International Development (AusAID) to develop a project to inform both men and women of the possibility of joint ownership (IFC n.d.). Research has shown that women in Vietnam have also suffered from a lack of awareness of their rights and of the advantages of including their names on LTCs (Weeks and Dang 2006).

Similarly, a recent study in Cambodia found that women's lack of knowledge of their land rights has hindered their ability to take advantage of and protect these rights (ADB 2004). In Cambodia, the Law on Marriage and Family gives equal rights to husband and wife to "use, obtain interests, and manage" their joint properties (properties obtained during marriage) as well as equal rights regarding properties they own individually (World Bank n.d.). The 2001 land law also sets out equal land rights for men and women. In practice, however, women in Cambodia have not fully benefited from this legal equality because of their low levels of literacy and lack of awareness of their land rights (ADB 2004).

Finally, in Indonesia, the Indonesian Marriage Law establishes the right to joint ownership of property purchased during marriage. However, there is evidence that 65 percent of the marital property certificates are issued in the husband's name (World Bank 2006b). This may be due, in part, to a lack of awareness of the possibility and advantages of registering jointly. Further sex-disaggregated research is needed to understand more precisely what women do and do not know about their rights.

## Credit

Access to credit is crucial for starting, sustaining, and growing viable enterprises. Several of the women profiled in a series of World Bank case studies of individual female entrepreneurs in the East Asia and Pacific region bring up problems in accessing credit on fair terms, revealing how widespread (and binding) this constraint is (World Bank 2010). At the regional level, East Asian and Pacific countries compare favorably with those in Sub-Saharan Africa, the Middle East and North Africa, and South Asia on all indicators but do less well than those in Europe and Central Asia as well as the Latin America and Caribbean regions.

This being said, the aggregated regional numbers are rather poor in absolute terms on all *Doing Business* credit indicators (World Bank 2009). As table 2.1 shows, for example, only 21.6 percent of adults in the East Asia and Pacific region are covered by either public credit registries or private credit bureaus. The region's Depth of Credit Information Index score is 1.9 out of 6.0; only Sub-Saharan Africa scores lower. Moreover, creditor rights have unsatisfactory protection, on average, as shown by the score of 5.7 out of 10 on the Strength of Legal Rights Index.

The access-to-credit indicators also show that country-specific performance varies widely within the region. Figure 2.3 compares the performance of East Asian and Pacific economies on a composite access-to-credit indicator (normalized score/100) based on two *Doing Business* indicators: the Depth of Credit Information Index and the Legal

**Table 2.1    Getting Credit: East Asia and Pacific vs. Other Regions**

| Region | Strength of Legal Rights Index[a] (0–10) | Depth of Credit Information Index[b] (0–6) | Public credit registry coverage (% of adults) | Private credit bureau coverage (% of adults) |
|---|---|---|---|---|
| East Asia and Pacific | 5.7 | 1.9 | 7.2 | 14.4 |
| Eastern Europe and Central Asia | 6.6 | 4.0 | 9.7 | 19.4 |
| Latin America and the Caribbean | 5.5 | 3.3 | 10.0 | 33.2 |
| Middle East & North Africa | 3.3 | 3.3 | 5.0 | 10.9 |
| South Asia | 5.3 | 2.1 | 0.8 | 3.3 |
| Sub-Saharan Africa | 4.6 | 1.5 | 2.4 | 4.5 |
| OECD member countries[c] | 6.8 | 4.9 | 8.8 | 59.6 |

*Source:* World Bank 2009.

a. The *Doing Business* Strength of Legal Rights Index measures the degree to which collateral and bankruptcy laws protect the rights of borrowers and lenders and thus facilitate lending.

b. The *Doing Business* Depth of Credit Information Index measures rules affecting the scope, accessibility, and quality of credit information available through either public or private credit registries. A score of 1.0 is assigned for each of the following six features of the public registry or the private credit bureau (or both): (1) Both positive credit information and negative information are distributed. (2) Data on both firms and individuals are distributed. (3) Data from retailers and utility companies are distributed to financial institutions. (4) More than two years of historical data are distributed. Registries that erase data on defaults as soon as they are repaid obtain a score of 0.0 for this indicator. (5) Data on loans below 1 percent of income per capita are distributed. A registry must have a minimum coverage of 1 percent of the adult population to score a 1.0 for this indicator. (6) Regulations guarantee borrowers the right to access their data in the largest registry in the economy.

c. OECD = Organisation for Economic Co-operation and Development. The 30 current OECD member countries include Australia, Austria, Belgium, Canada, the Czech Republic, Denmark, Finland, France, Germany, Greece, Hungary, Iceland, Ireland, Italy, Japan, the Republic of Korea, Luxembourg, Mexico, the Netherlands, New Zealand, Norway, Poland, Portugal, the Slovak Republic, Spain, Sweden, Switzerland, Turkey, the United Kingdom, and the United States.

**Figure 2.3   Composite Credit Indicator, Selected East Asian and Pacific Economies**

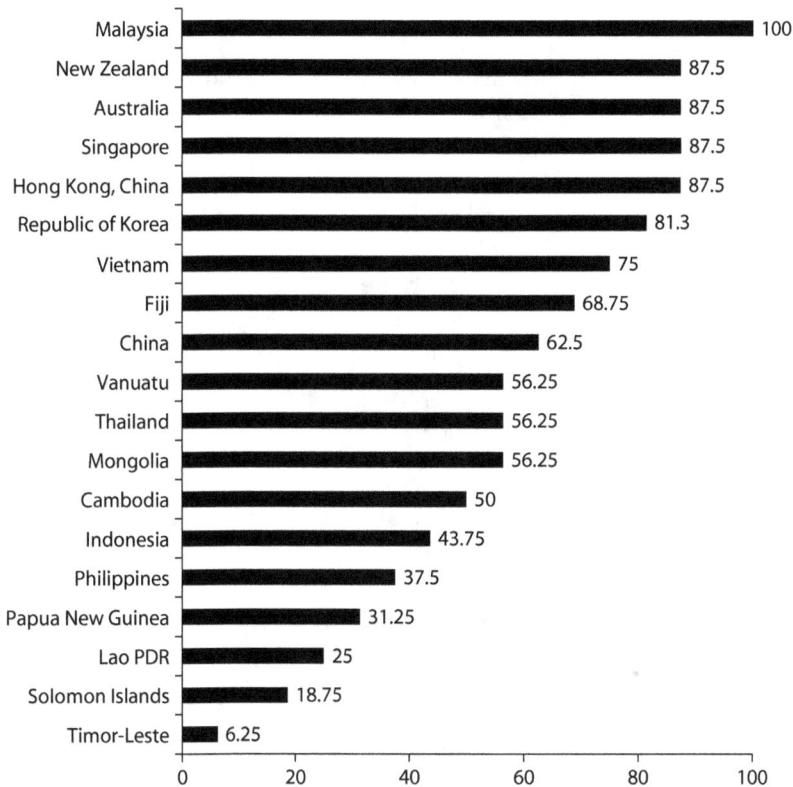

Source: World Bank 2009.
Note: Composite Credit Indicator score is calculated by summing the Legal Rights Index and the Depth of Credit Informations Index data by country and then normalizing the combined score out of 100. For definitions of the Legal Rights Index and Depth of Credit Information Index, see notes a. and b. to table 2.1. Data are not disaggregated by gender.

Rights Index (EIU forthcoming). Although neither index is disaggregated by sex, each is useful in assessing women's access to credit. The composition of the Depth of Credit Information Index reflects some gender concerns, even though the data itself are not disaggregated by sex. The scores shown in figure 2.3 reflect the following:

- Whether both positive credit information (for example, loan amounts and patterns of on-time payments) and negative information (for example, late payments and the number and amount of defaults and bankruptcies) is distributed. Women benefit from the availability of positive data because research suggests that women tend to have excellent repayment rates (see ADB 2006a, for example).

- Whether data on both firms and individuals are distributed. Fewer women than men own firms, so credit data on individuals are important to the many women who operate as sole proprietors.
- Whether data on loans below 1 percent of income per capita are distributed. Women may benefit from this data because they tend to have smaller firms than men and are highly concentrated in the microenterprise sector.
- Whether data from retailers, trade creditors or utility companies, and financial institutions are distributed. Women benefit disproportionately from this information because they are less likely to have prior loan histories. This category also includes data from microfinance institutions—of which women are the main customers.

The Legal Rights Index collects information on whether businesses can use movable assets as collateral while keeping possession of the assets, and whether any financial institution accepts such assets as collateral (which may disproportionately benefit women who may not have immovable assets—for example, land—as collateral). The East Asian and Pacific countries fall into three main groups regarding their performance on this indicator:

- The region's advanced economies, along with Fiji, which all score well
- Four middle-income countries (Cambodia, China, Thailand, and Vietnam) that post satisfactory performance with room for improvement
- Indonesia, Lao PDR, the Philippines, and the Pacific island states, which perform weakly relative to the region's other countries. World Bank case studies of female entrepreneurs in the Philippines and Indonesia strongly confirm that access to credit is a significant constraint to doing business in their countries (see boxes 2.1 and 3.1).

Country-level data confirms the seriousness of credit constraints in several countries in the region.

### Lao PDR

- Lao PDR ranks 150th out of 183 economies for the *Doing Business* Depth of Credit Information indicator (World Bank 2009).
- Twenty-five percent of firms cite access to finance as a major constraint to doing business (World Bank 2007b).

- Only 10 percent of firms have overdraft facilities, compared with 71 percent in Malaysia, 44 percent in Vietnam, and 19 percent in Indonesia (World Bank 2007b).
- Microfirms in Lao PDR listed access to credit as the most significant constraint to doing business (World Bank 2007b).

### China

- Access to finance for small and medium enterprises (SMEs) varies considerably among the different regions, from 51.2 percent in Bohai to only 24.8 percent in the Northeast, where nonperforming loans to state-owned enterprises (SOEs) make it more difficult for banks to lend to SMEs (World Bank 2006a).[1]

### Pacific Island countries

- While a survey of Pacific Island countries (Fiji, Papua New Guinea, Samoa, Tonga, and Vanuatu) indicated that a large majority of firms could get loans in most of the countries, Papua New Guinea was an exception, with only a 35 percent success rate for those who applied for a loan (IFC 2003).
- Even where loans were obtained, they appear to have been insufficient, with most firms in Papua New Guinea, Samoa, and Vanuatu saying they needed more financing despite having short- or long-term loans (IFC 2003).
- Samoa and Tonga have a high proportion of female business ownership in aggregate, but the ratio of female to male owners declines dramatically by business segment size; women own proportionally fewer SMEs than microenterprises (IFC 2003). One possible reason for this ownership pattern is that women lack sufficient access to the capital they need for business expansion.

Reasons for credit-access constraints vary across the region. Constraints emerge on both the demand and supply side for all entrepreneurs, whether they are women or men. However, research is needed to determine the extent to which (1) *on the demand side,* women are less aware than men of (and so have less demand for) the formal sector financial products available; and (2) *on the supply side,* whether there are systematic differences in the amounts and commercial terms of credit offered to women and men with the same borrower profiles.

While these constraints limit entrepreneurship among both men and women in the region, evidence suggests that they disproportionately affect women. In Indonesia, for example, one study reveals that just over one out of three women have problems getting loans, compared with just one out of four men (IFC 2006a). Moreover, Indonesian women make up roughly the same the proportion of microcredit customers as they have for the past 20 years, suggesting that the situation is not improving (World Bank 2006b).

The ADB Country Gender Assessment for China also suggests that women find it harder to get credit except where microcredit institutions specifically target women (ADB 2006a). When they do get these loans, they have higher success rates than men for their activities and for repayments. By 2002, one microcredit lender in China had granted credit to 1,481 laid-off women; their repayment success was 97 percent and business success 100 percent (ADB 2006a). While one lender's repayment rate is not enough evidence to generalize about the creditworthiness of women entrepreneurs, it does support the case for improving credit information, particularly about women's credit and repayment behavior with microfinance. Better information may help eliminate, or at least reduce, the greater difficulties women appear to have in getting loans.

Understanding which constraints bind most strongly when it comes to women's access to finance is limited by the fact that most access-to-finance statistics are not sex-disaggregated. However, qualitative and quantitative evidence suggests some common factors. The most significant of these include demand-side constraints stemming from a lack of information for women about the financing options available to them. Other crucial factors are women's lower financial literacy; widespread persistence of discriminatory local practices (for example, some financial providers' insistence on husbands' cosignatures on loan applications, even when not legally required); high financing costs; inflexibility of formal financial institutions toward the needs of small and informal businesses (many of which are female owned), including an emphasis on land as collateral; and women's time poverty, which makes them less able to negotiate the complex procedures necessary to get loans.

First (and echoing the analysis of land rights above), women entrepreneurs are often unaware of their rights or of the credit options available to their businesses. The World Bank's investment climate assessment for Lao PDR indicates that many entrepreneurs in the country are not well informed about the financial options open to them (World Bank 2007b). More research is needed to determine whether informational deficits are relatively more severe for women and to understand the impact of these deficits on their credit-seeking behavior.

*Second, even where women have equal rights and are aware of those rights, customary practices may override the law.* In China, for example, women often must show their husbands' identity cards to apply for credit (ADB 2006a). Similarly in the Philippines, women often must have their husbands' signatures on loan documents (ADB and World Bank 2008). This means that despite formal legal equality, Chinese and Filipino women cannot get credit on the same terms as men. A case study of a Filipino female entrepreneur shows that even where previously discriminatory law has been reformed (the Philippines' 1992 Republic Act 7192 ended the legal need for spousal consent for women applying for credit), implementation can take years to catch up (see box 2.1). High income status is no guarantee of equality; in another case study, a Korean entrepreneur reports that her initial attempts to start a business, despite her business acumen and extensive network of social contacts, were unsuccessful because of gender discrimination regarding requirements for proof of creditworthiness (World Bank 2010). Women, it is reported, must have a longer track record and more credit or assets relative to men. In Indonesia, there is evidence of substantial bias against married women earning their own incomes. Because regulations do not permit the assignment of tax numbers to married women, they are forced to use their husbands'. This makes it harder for them to engage in financial transactions such as opening a checking account or, by extension, applying for credit (ADB 2006b).

*Third, the characteristics of women-led businesses, many of which are small, also constrain access to finance.* There is some rigorous, and much anecdotal, evidence that women tend to lead smaller enterprises. In Indonesia, 85 percent of female entrepreneurs own small-scale businesses (IFC 2006a), whereas a Lao PDR study showed that women owned 63 percent of SMEs but that the SMEs owned by men tended to be larger (Siliphong, Khampoui, and Mihyo 2005). Size matters because risk-averse financial institutions perceive smaller businesses to be riskier. Beck, Laeven, and Maksimovic (2004) used data from the World Bank's World Business Environment Survey to show that, on a global level, a firm's size is the most significant factor that determines access to credit (with smaller firms having poorer access). Additionally, one global study of SMEs indicates that access to credit is, along with inflation, the most significant barrier to growth of the SME sector (Ayyagari, Beck, and Demirgüç-Kunt 2003). Because of perceived higher risks, banks are often unwilling to lend to small businesses or to adapt services to their particular needs. One example of inflexibility on this score is Chinese banks' unwillingness to adjust the collateral requirements that many SMEs cannot fulfill (World Bank 2007a).

Country-level evidence from the region confirms the relationship of firm size to credit access. It is estimated that only 25 percent of small-scale businesses in Indonesia, for instance, have access to credit from formal financial institutions (World Bank 2006b). A survey of SMEs in Pacific Island countries indicates that business owners in Papua New Guinea perceive lenders as unwilling to lend to small businesses (IFC 2003). Women entrepreneurs in Vietnam also cited, as a major barrier, the inflexibility of traditional financial institutions in adapting to the needs of small businesses (IFC 2006b). Consequently, in Vietnam as well as in other East Asian and Pacific countries, women business owners are more likely to use informal sources of finance as getting a bank loan is generally feasible only for large businesses (IFC 2006b). Banks are not only unwilling to lend to smaller business, but also set credit conditions that smaller businesses, cannot meet.

*Fourth, on the supply side, collateral-based banking systems constrain access.* The traditional emphasis on land as collateral is likely to disproportionately affect women not only because of their smaller average business size, but also because women generally have poorer access to land and property, and, as such, are less able to get credit through formal channels (ADB and World Bank 2008). Although part of the solution lies in gender-equal land rights (and sufficient implementation of these rights), developing credit systems that rely less on collateral is also important. The Philippine Department of Trade and Industry (DTI) acknowledged this in its SME Development Plan 2004–2010, which identified an overemphasis on collateral as a major barrier to SMEs' access to credit. The constraints caused by a collateral-based lending system are also highlighted in a case study of a Filipino business woman, who, drawing on her own experience in starting a business and facing a complex and difficult credit environment, has helped other female entrepreneurs by establishing a franchise business model (see box 2.1).

*Fifth, the sheer cost of financing can also constrain the smaller enterprises led by women.* While there is considerable variation across countries, the cost of financing appears to be particularly high in the region. Surveys of firms' own views about the constraints on their growth reveal that high interest rates are perceived to be very binding. The largest proportion of firms in the region (72.5 percent) cite interest rates as a "major" or "moderate" financing constraint compared with other constraints (Kaufmann, Batra, and Stone 2003). Interest rates in Lao PDR are particularly high when compared to regional neighbors, such as Thailand. Although informal money lenders provide additional avenues for credit, the high risk involved and a lack of legal recourse mean that interest rates can be as much as 50 percent per day (World Bank 2007b). This finding is echoed in Mongolia, where the cost of finance is a severe problem and the required value of collateral to loans is higher than in any other country—as a consequence, less than one-third of firms have a bank loan (World Bank 2007c). Such costs are likely to affect the smallest businesses the most because they tend to operate close to the edge, with little room to maneuver in terms of costs. They also tend to be owned by poorer people with less access to collateral. More consistent, sex-disaggregated data on the average financing costs faced by women, compared with those faced by men, are needed to understand completely whether these costs reflect a consistent gender bias.

*Finally, the complexity of financing procedures appears to be a particular concern among female entrepreneurs in the East Asia and Pacific region.* Indeed, in one survey of Vietnamese businesswomen, the highest proportion of respondents (29 percent) rated complicated procedures as the most significant barrier to obtaining credit (IFC 2006c). In another study in Vietnam, Han and Baumgarte (2000) also found that entrepreneurs had a negative perception of loan application procedures. And in a survey of Pacific Island SMEs, firms in Fiji, Samoa, and Tonga identified "paperwork" as the main problem in accessing finance (IFC 2003). The time-consuming nature of dealing with complex procedures may be especially constraining for women, who tend to take on the largest share of household and family responsibilities.

Improving the credit supply side is a long-term process, which accompanies the general process of economic development. In the medium term, however, countries can develop and implement innovative policies to increase financial access for entrepreneurs, particularly in the medium, small, and micro sectors. Two possibilities for such innovation are leasing and franchising.

The case study of a female entrepreneur in the Philippines demonstrates clearly why the franchising business model can particularly benefit women entrepreneurs. Pacita Juan's coffee franchising business has been win-win for both her and her franchisees. For Juan, franchising offered a different way to scale up in a credit-constrained environment. For her franchisees, Figaro Coffee offers an established brand, know-how in navigating complex business procedures (including subnational differences in entry regulations), and a guarantee for their bank loans (see box 2.1).

More generally, the franchisor's loan guarantee can help women enter the business world by easing credit constraints (especially where banks require long track records for a loan, something that many women lack when they are starting out). Franchising also provides an established brand to encourage early sales, helps franchisees to navigate business entry and licensing requirements, and provides targeted business development services.

Leasing, another alternative to collateral-based lending, can also be a catalyst for women led enterprises. Leasing is especially important where women own little immovable property (such as land) and where traditional credit is collateral based. It helps businesses gain immediate access to capital assets for starting or expanding production. The businesses repay the value of the asset, with interest, in installments with flexible repayment schedules that are calibrated to anticipated cash-flow patterns. Leasing can thus allow new businesses with limited start-up capital (such as the Figaro Coffee franchises) but good short-term cash-flow potential to start operating immediately.

Little systematic research has been done on the impact, costs, and benefits of leasing as opposed to other financial products to increase women's access to finance in East Asian and Pacific countries. However, research from elsewhere has shown that leasing offers significant potential for women entrepreneurs. In Uganda, for example, the introduction of a leasing product appreciably increased women's access to finance.[2]

### Labor

Labor laws and regulations are important determinants of the economic opportunities available to women workers. These regulations also indirectly affect female participation in entrepreneurship; if women have less opportunity to participate equally with men in the labor market, they are less able to progress to senior management positions and to pick up the skills to become successful entrepreneurs. The Global Entrepreneurship Monitor's "Report on Women and Entrepreneurship" (Allen and others 2008) shows that, globally, women who are employed are three to four times more likely than unemployed women to engage in entrepreneurship, suggesting that employment facilitates access to resources, social capital, and ideas that are crucial to entrepreneurship. A lack of opportunities in the labor market arguably may also force women to become entrepreneurs to make a living. However, although a dearth of employment opportunities may increase the absolute number of female entrepreneurs, women who are forced into entrepreneurship in this way are less likely to have the management and business skills required for success.

One way to measure progress on equality in labor regulation is to examine countries' progress in enforcing their commitments (where they exist) to International Labour Organization (ILO) Convention 100 (covering equal pay) and ILO Convention 111 (covering nondiscrimination). Table 2.2 shows the ratification status of both conventions among East Asian and Pacific countries as of 2009.

While ratification is one step, implementation and enforcement of convention commitments clearly matter as well. The persistence of a gender earnings gap in all economies in the region shows that implementation has lagged behind ratification (see figure 2.4).

Whereas an earnings gap is only a partial proxy for wage inequality (given potentially systematic differences between the regularity and duration of employment for women versus men), any differences in hours worked are unlikely to completely explain the size of an earnings gap. Thus, it is likely that these sizeable earnings gaps are at least partially driven by wage inequality between men and women.

To ascertain how well countries have progressed on implementing their convention commitments, we combine the two scores (for Convention

**Table 2.2    ILO Convention Ratifications, East Asian and Pacific Countries**

| Country | Convention 100 | Convention 111 |
|---|---|---|
| Australia | √ | √ |
| Cambodia | √ | √ |
| China | √ | √ |
| Indonesia | √ | √ |
| Laos PDR | √ | √ |
| Korea, Rep. of | √ | √ |
| Malaysia | √ | X |
| Mongolia | √ | √ |
| New Zealand | √ | √ |
| Papua New Guinea | √ | √ |
| Philippines | √ | √ |
| Singapore | √ | X |
| Solomon Islands | X | X |
| Thailand | √ | X |
| Timor-Leste | X | X |
| Vietnam | √ | √ |

*Source:* International Labour Organization National Labour Legislation Database (NATLEX).
*Note:* √ = ratified; X = not ratified. ILO Convention 100 calls for equal pay for men and women. ILO Convention 111 calls for nondiscrimination in employment.

**Figure 2.4    Female-Male Earning Gaps, Selected East Asian and Pacific Economies**

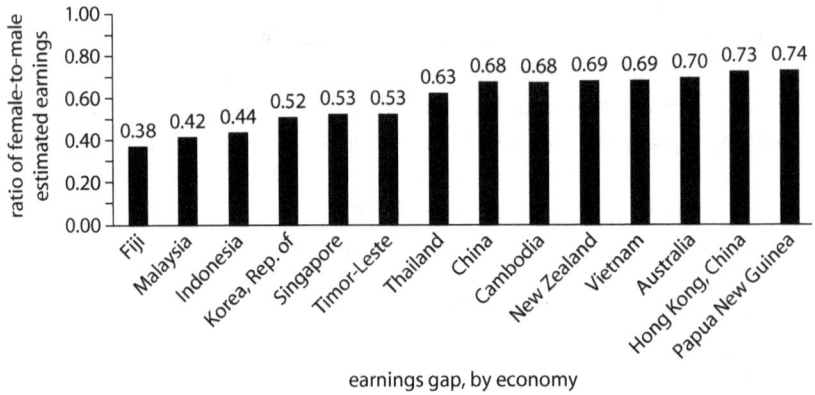

earnings gap, by economy

*Sources:* United Nations Development Programme (UNDP) Gender and Development Index (GDI), latest available data, 1997–2007.

*Note:* Data are calculated based on female-to-male ratios of estimated earned income for the most recent year available between 1996 and 2007. Following the methodology implemented in the calculation of the GDI, the income component has been scaled downward for economies whose income exceeds the maximum goalpost gross domestic product per capita value of 40,000 (PPP US$). For more details, see http://hdr.undp.org/en/statistics/tn1. PPP = purchasing power parity.

100 and Convention 111) used in an EIU analysis[3] and normalize to scores out of a possible 100 (where 100 indicates best possible compliance on both categories) (EIU, forthcoming). Figure 2.5 shows the composite scores, with Australia and New Zealand doing substantially better than their counterparts in the region.

Significantly, the less-developed, export-oriented countries receive markedly lower scores, particularly with regard to enforcement of ILO Convention 100 on equal pay. Some have argued that, in those countries, workforce segregation—that has placed women in labor-intensive jobs in export-oriented businesses and is paying them less than men for their work—has helped Asian economies to reduce the per-unit labor costs of export goods (Seguino 2000).

This view, which suggests that wage inequality has helped spur Asia's export-driven economic growth, does not necessarily contradict the idea that gender equality in terms of greater female workforce participation has also contributed to the region's economic growth. It does suggest, however, that women continue to encounter discrimination and that they may find that social attitudes and norms make it harder for them to reach their potential as employees or as entrepreneurs. Seguino also points out that women were singled out to bear the burden of Asia's push for export

**Figure 2.5   Enforcement of ILO Convention 100 (equal pay) and 111
(nondiscrimination in employment) in Selected East Asian and Pacific Economies**

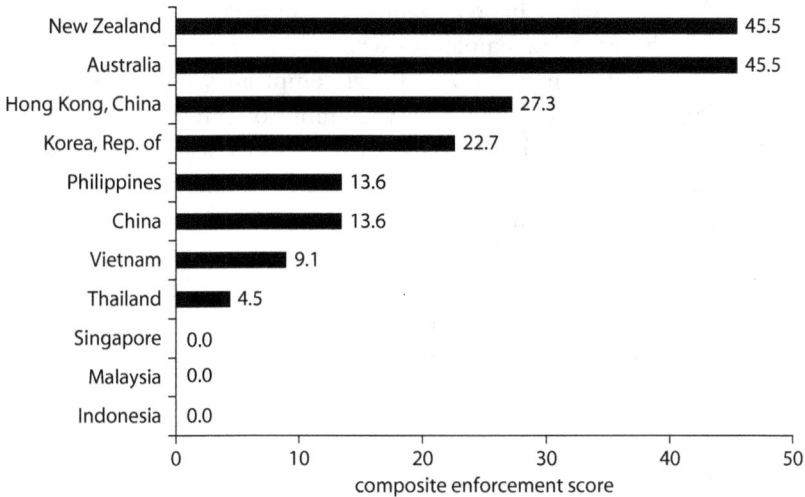

New Zealand 45.5
Australia 45.5
Hong Kong, China 27.3
Korea, Rep. of 22.7
Philippines 13.6
China 13.6
Vietnam 9.1
Thailand 4.5
Singapore 0.0
Malaysia 0.0
Indonesia 0.0

composite enforcement score

*Source:* EIU, forthcoming.
*Note:* For definitions and metrics of ILO Conventions 100 and 111, see endnote 3 in chapter 2. Enforcement relates to implementation of the following: (1) government policy and organization or committee to promote convention principles; (2) principle of equality in remuneration in practice; (3) principle of equal values in practice; (4) job appraisal or evaluation mechanisms; (5) cooperation with workers and employers' organizations to involve them in achieving wage equality; and (6) law inspection and enforcement mechanisms.

success, perhaps because placing the burden on men would have risked social unrest (Seguino 2000).

On the higher end of the ILO Convention composite scores, Australia provides a good example of how equal labor laws require effective watchdog and facilitation agencies for effective enforcement. For example, the Equal Opportunity for Women in the Workplace Agency (EOWA) works with employers to advance women in business and requires that firms with more than 100 employees institute workforce programs and report their progress annually. Today, 1 million Australian women work for organizations that report to EOWA, constituting close to one-fourth of the country's female workforce. EOWA's flagship citation program, Employer of Choice for Women (EOCFW), attracts media and corporate attention alike, giving companies incentives to earn the citation by adopting women-friendly workplace policies.[4]

The agency seems to have had a definite impact on the business community: The number of organizations seeking the EOCFW citation has more than doubled since it was established in 2001, citation holders regularly use the logo on their recruitment advertisements, and competitors within industries have followed each other in acquiring the citation (Greater London Authority 2007). In organizations that have failed to treat men and women equally, individual employees who believe they have been subject to sex discrimination may file an official complaint with the Australian Human Rights and Equal Opportunity Commission (HREOC).[5]

Whereas initiatives such as EOWA's can play a significant role in advancing women-friendly workplace policies, tackling cultural barriers is much trickier. Such normative barriers to women at work can restrict the extent to which commitments, such as ILO 100, are met in actual business and employment practices. Even in the developed Republic of Korea, for example, being a woman in business and in the labor force is not easy, as the female entrepreneur profiled in box 2.2 attests.

**Box 2.2**

## Case Study Excerpt

### Republic of Korea: Sung-Joo Kim
CEO, SungJoo Group & MCM Group

In the Republic of Korea, rapid economic growth has not always translated into equal "rules-of-the-game" for women entrepreneurs, who comprise only 19 percent of all Korean business owners and have a low labor force participation rate of only 39 percent. Although Sung-Joo recognized the business potential of high-end fashion in Asia early on, establishing her business was hampered by difficult business start-up procedures and traditional notions of a woman's place in Korean society.

Upon completing her studies in the United States, Sung-Joo returned to the Republic of Korea to start her business. However, Sung-Joo had not bargained on the difficulties she would encounter as a woman entrepreneur in Korea's male-dominated business world. Despite years of increases in women's education, patriarchal notions have remained prevalent in Korean society, according to which men are expected to dominate the public and women the domestic sphere. Gender discrimination proved to be a particular obstacle for Sung-Joo when she first embarked on her business career.

Securing start-up capital was an early stumbling block. As she remarks, "loan managers were interested in supporting the business plan on paper, but turned

*(continued)*

**Box 2.2** *(continued)*

me down after they met the woman behind the business concept. Even today, gender discrimination continues with unequal requirements by banks for proof of creditworthiness." This situation was previously exacerbated by a high minimum paid up capital requirement, which encouragingly has since been abolished. Coming from a wealthy Korean family, Sung-Joo was ultimately able to turn to her businessman father for a start-up loan, a luxury not available to most potential entrepreneurs.

Sung-Joo also encountered problems with the Republic of Korea's complex business registration regime; a total of eight different procedures are required; it was even more cumbersome when Sung-Joo began in business in the 1990s. Given her frustration with the cumbersome procedures, Sung-Joo decided to pay an incorporation expert to ensure her new company was in regulatory compliance. Despite this expert assistance, it took several months to register her company in 1990. For those who cannot afford to hire an expert to help them manage the process, registration procedures can be even more daunting. These obstacles make starting a business especially difficult for women, who are less likely to have the needed money, time, or contacts to navigate the process.

*Sources:* World Bank 2009, 2010.

Such de facto discrimination is found in several developing countries in the region. In China, increasing unemployment has created tensions in the labor market, apparently exacerbating the tendency toward gender discrimination in employment. Reportedly, some job postings openly express a preference for male employees in many areas. Recent female graduates with good qualifications are often less likely to be hired than males with lower credentials (Li and others 2002; ADB 2006a). More systematic research would shed light on the degree and severity of such discrimination in the workplace as well as its dimensions: glass ceilings in management, unequal hiring practices, de facto restrictions on job types, and so forth.

## Internal Assets: Human Capital and Time

The success of enterprises is partly a function of the skills and time of those who run them. If women lack the right business skills, they are unlikely to make a success of their businesses, no matter how attractive the business environment. Moreover, if they lack the *time* to properly manage and develop their businesses and to navigate complex procedures, often because of the tension between their reproductive and productive roles (and their traditional role as caregivers for the young and elderly), their chances for success are also diminished.

### Human Capital and Vocational Skills

Education is highly correlated with economic outcomes for women, as suggested by figure 2.6, which depicts a simple global correlation between female literacy rates and the ratio of women to men who are paid employees. The correlation remains strongly positive, even when controlling for GDP per capita.

Encouragingly, the East Asia and Pacific region seems to be doing well in terms of adult female literacy rates. On this front, as figure 2.7 shows, the region has been outperforming the Middle East and North Africa, South Asia, and Sub-Saharan Africa regions, although it also includes some significantly underperforming outliers: Cambodia, Lao PDR, and Papua New Guinea.

*Vocational and technical training and education.* Literacy rates are obviously only part of the story; vocational and technical training also affect women's business success. While the region is generally performing well on female educational indexes, evidence suggests that women have poorer business skills than men and suffer from a lack of business-relevant education (Weeks and Dang 2006; Kantor 2001; ADB 2006a). Among the primary concerns that the region's women entrepreneurs have raised in surveys is a lack of necessary skills for business success. Their apparently lower levels of entrepreneurial competencies have various explanations, but many seem related to women's inferior position in the labor market (particularly their concentration in informal, low-skilled, and nonbusiness-related work), along with societal biases that exacerbate the situation.

First, women have less access to vocational and technical training (Weeks and Dang 2006; Kantor 2001). Figure 2.8 shows the proportions of female and male vocational and technical secondary-level students as percentages of female and male total secondary-level enrollment in countries for which recent World Bank *EdStats* data are available.[6] Except in Australia, the region's women are not enrolled in great numbers in vocational or technical training. Moreover, men have greater proportional enrollment in all countries except Cambodia, China, New Zealand, and Vietnam. Overall,

**Figure 2.6    Global Correlation of Adult Female-to-Male Literacy Ratio and Female-Male Employment Ratio, Selected East Asian and Pacific Economies Highlighted**

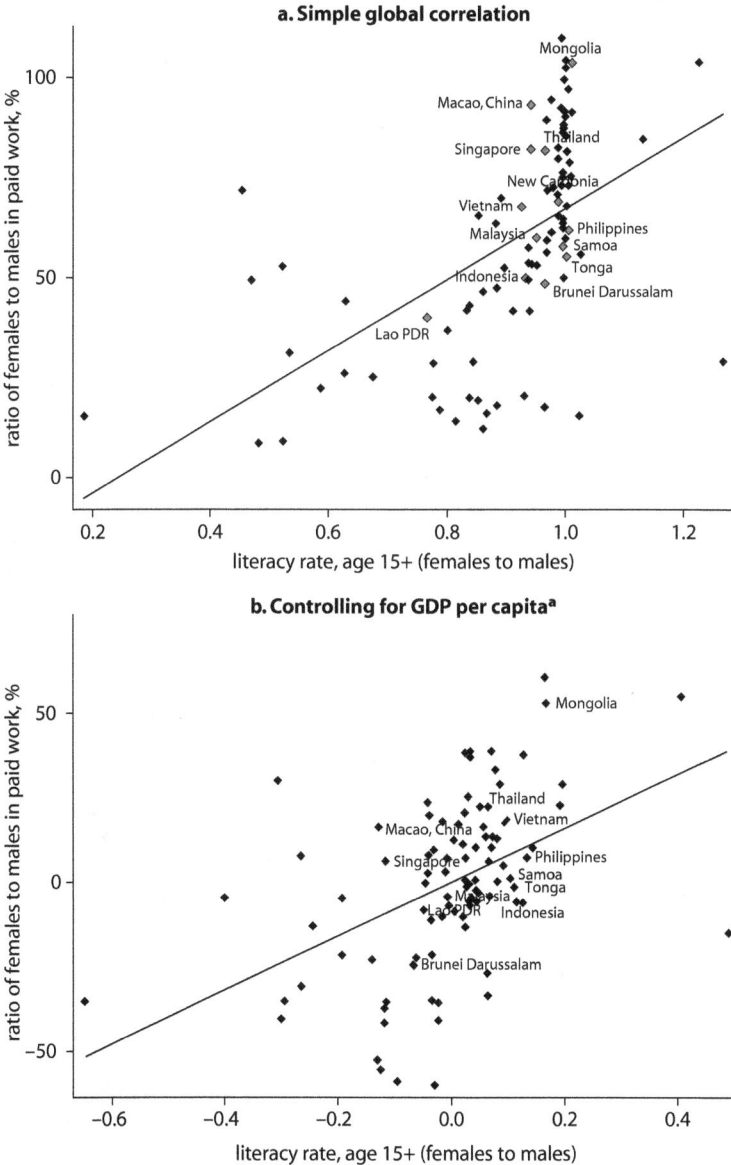

**a. Simple global correlation**

**b. Controlling for GDP per capita[a]**

*Sources:* World Bank *Gender Stats*; International Labour Organization Key Indicators of the Labour Market Database, latest available data, 1998–2008.
*Note:* GDP = gross national product; ILO = International Labour Organization.
a. coef = 79.353006, se = 15.721894, t = 5.05.

**Figure 2.7    Adult Female Literacy Rates, by Region**

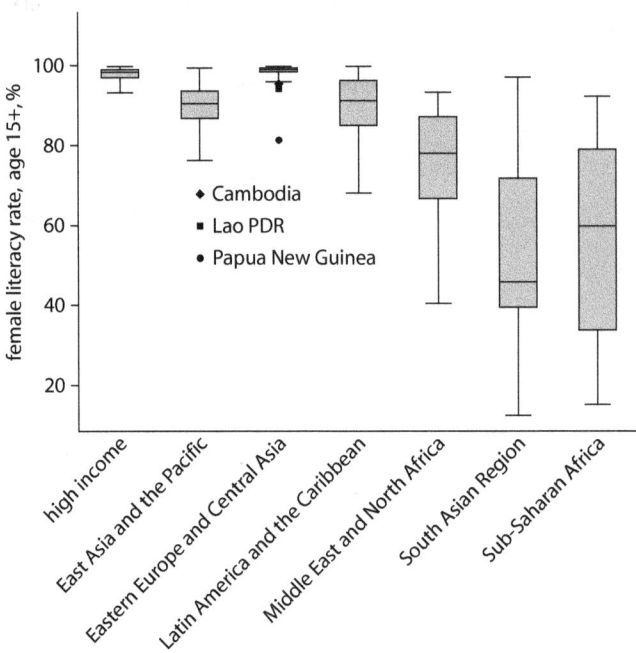

Source: World Development Indicators, latest available data, 1998–2008.
Note: Boxes show 25th to 75th percentiles. Bars within the boxes show the median value. End bars show
the upper and lower adjacent values. Regions are defined according to World Bank Group Classification.
"High income" designates all those countries (regardless of geography, except if they are in the Middle East)
whose gross national income (GNI) per capita (Atlas Method) in 2008 was greater than US$11,906. Countries
that are geographically in the Middle East but whose GNI per capita meets the high income threshold are
nevertheless classified as in the Middle East and North Africa region for the purposes of the analysis.
High-income countries in that region are significant outliers, and the normal relationship between
high-income status and gender outcomes does not hold. Including them in the high income category would
thus distort the aggregate results.

the East Asia and Pacific region performs only marginally better than the Sub-Saharan Africa region and worse than high-income and Latin American and Caribbean regions on this indicator.

Second, lower retirement ages for women (in effect in China, Lao PDR, and Vietnam) can negatively affect women's access to training and promotion opportunities and therefore to economic advancement. There is evidence, for example, that training policies are skewed toward men's interests as a direct result of lower retirement ages for women. In fact, World Bank research suggests that the glaring gap between men and women's statutory pensionable retirement ages in Vietnam results in women earning 12 percent and 13 percent less than men in rural and urban Vietnam, respectively. Under Vietnamese training policies, the

## Figure 2.8    Access to Vocational and Technical Training by Gender

### a. Males and females enrolled

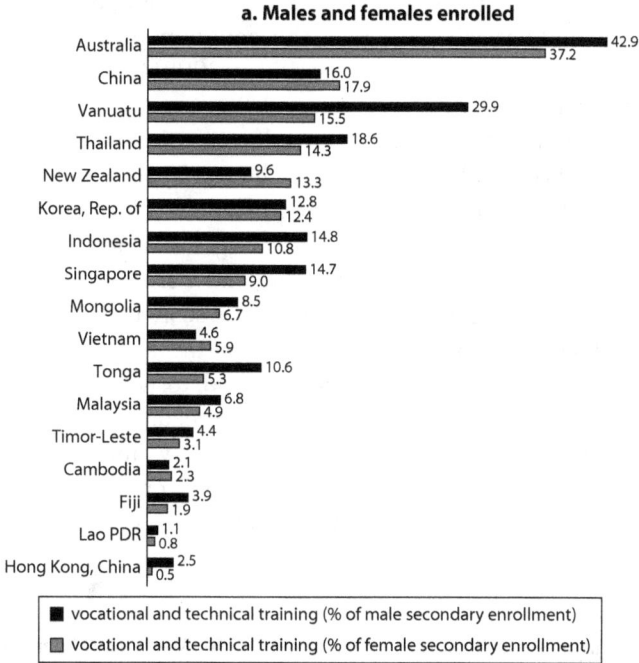

- vocational and technical training (% of male secondary enrollment)
- vocational and technical training (% of female secondary enrollment)

### b. Vocational and technical education, females, by region

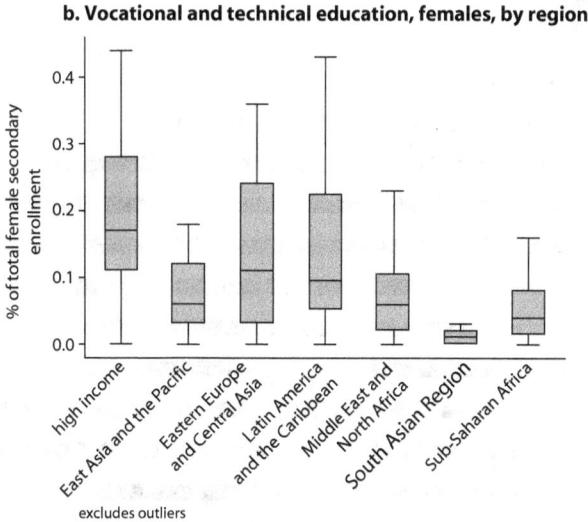

excludes outliers

*Source:* World Bank EdStats, latest available data, 1998–2008.
*Note:* Boxes show 25th to 75th percentiles. Bars within the boxes show the median value. End bars show the upper and lower adjacent values. Regions are defined according to World Bank Group Classification. "High income" designates all those countries (regardless of geography, except if they are in the Middle East) whose gross national income per capita (Atlas Method) in 2008 was greater than US$11,906. For definition of geographic and high-income regions, see note to figure 2.7.

cut-off age for promotions and training is five years lower for women than for men (Sabharwal and Huong 2007). World Bank researchers hope these findings will influence the government of Vietnam as it revises the Vietnamese Labor Code (Pham 2008).

Figure 2.9 shows how East Asian and Pacific economies perform on equalizing retirement ages, based on qualitative assessments by EIU analysts (EIU forthcoming). A score of 7 (achieved by most of the countries surveyed) indicates that there is no difference between men's and women's statutory pensionable retirement ages. A score of 6 (Australia) indicates a difference of up to three years, and a score of 4 (China) indicates a difference of up to five years. Finally, a score of 1 (Vietnam) indicates a difference of five or more years in the statutory pensionable retirement age and that the difference is mandatory.

A case study of a Chinese female entrepreneur expressed forcefully how differential retirement age regulations affect women. Surveys by the company of media entrepreneur Yang Lan have consistently highlighted Chinese women's concerns about this issue: Lower retirement ages hurt

**Figure 2.9    Differential Statutory Retirement Ages for Men and Women, Selected East Asian and Pacific Economies**

*EIU 7-point scale*

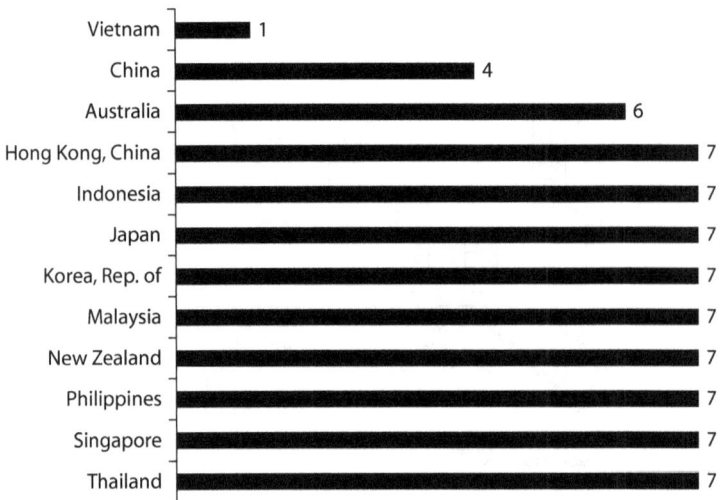

*Source:* EIU, forthcoming.
*Note:* EIU = Economist Intelligence Unit. On EIU scale of 1 to 7, 1 = mandatory statutory pensionable retirement age is five or more years earlier for women than for men. 7 = no difference.

women's opportunities for career progression and reduce their final pension pay. "Earlier retirement ages for women may have made sense when most of the jobs relied on physical labor, but it doesn't apply to the current situation anymore. At the age of 55, many women, just like their male counterparts, are at the prime of their experiences and management skills," says Yang, chief executive and cofounder, Sun Media Holdings China, and owner of HerVillage.com, China's largest online portal for professional women (World Bank 2010).

Further constraining women's ability to develop their human capital is the lower probability that they will reach senior positions, in which they could better improve their business skills. World Bank Enterprise Surveys suggest that men predominate in senior decision-making positions throughout the region, with women occupying only 6.4 percent of senior positions in the private sector. Country-level data on the proportion of women in administrative and managerial positions, shown in figure 2.10, show that women continue to be at a disadvantage in pursuing these positions. Moreover, the East Asia and Pacific region seems to perform less well than other regions on this indicator, as the lower graph in the figure shows.

This means that potential women entrepreneurs in the region are less likely to gain the same level of management experience as men. Country-level studies also indicate that women are concentrated in lower-level positions. In Vietnam, for example, even in sectors where women dominate, they rarely hold top decision-making positions. In Vietnam's education sector, women represent 71 percent of workers, yet men head almost all educational institutions (World Bank 2006c). In Indonesia, across all sectors of the economy, women occupy only 14 percent of senior positions, compared with 86 percent for men (World Bank 2006b). Similarly, in Lao PDR, which has one of the highest female economic participation rates in the world (more than 70 percent), women in the formal sector are concentrated in low-skilled jobs (Siliphong, Khampoui, and Mihyo 2005).

In addition, women's business skills may be negatively affected by girls' tendency to study only those school subjects linked to traditional ideas of women's role in society. If women are to be more successful in the formal labor market or have a better chance of becoming successful entrepreneurs, it is important that they study in areas that are relevant to running a business. Research in Indonesia by the International Finance Corporation (IFC) noted that women were still pressured to study subjects that would prepare them for domestic functions (IFC 2006a). Likewise, in Thailand

**Figure 2.10    Proportion of Administrative and Managerial Positions Held by Women**

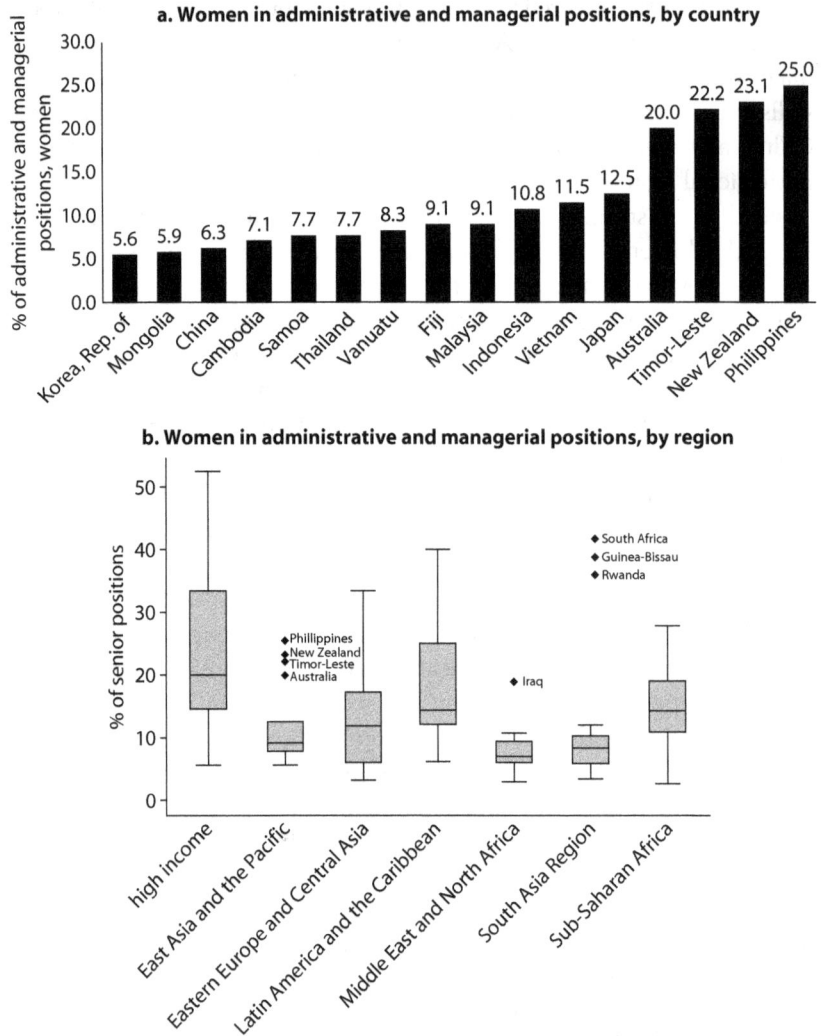

**a. Women in administrative and managerial positions, by country**

**b. Women in administrative and managerial positions, by region**

*Source:* World Bank *Gender Stats*, latest available data, 2002–08.
*Note:* For definition of geographic and high-income regions, see note to figure 2.7.

there seems to be a mismatch between the subjects that girls study and employers' demands (ADB 1998). Evidence of societal bias also exists in other countries, such as Vietnam, where school textbooks perpetuate gender stereotypes and where women in public sector roles are steered toward "soft" social sectors and away from "hard" areas such as business (World Bank 2006c).

Social biases affect not only the type of work perceived to be suitable for women, but also the degree to which women are generally accepted in the workforce. A World Values survey reveals that, in many countries in the region, people believe that employers should prefer male job applicants during high-unemployment periods (EIU, forthcoming). In Indonesia, Malaysia, the Philippines, and Thailand, more than half the survey respondents agreed that men have more of a right to a job when jobs are scarce (see figure 2.11).

The global data based on this survey question suggest that attitudes matter in determining women's economic opportunity in the labor market. Figures 2.12 and 2.13 depict how the female-to-male ratios of paid workers and female-to-male earnings ratios, respectively, correlate to the percentages of survey respondents who agreed that men should be preferred for jobs when jobs are scarce. The relationship is negative in both cases, even when controlling for GDP per capita.

In other words, the more people in a country who think that men should have the first shot at jobs, the more one might expect to find

**Figure 2.11   Social Attitudes toward Value of Men's and Women's Employment, Selected East Asian and Pacific Economies**

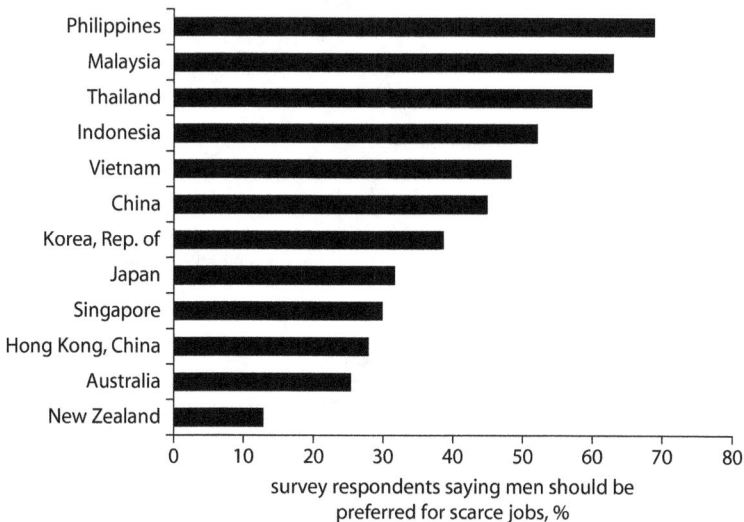

survey respondents saying men should be preferred for scarce jobs, %

*Source:* World Values Survey, 1981–2008, http://www.worldvaluessurvey.org/.
*Note:* Figure displays the percentage of respondents in each economy who agreed with the following statement: "When jobs are scarce, men should have more right to a job than women."

**Figure 2.12    Global Correlation of Attitudes toward Female Work and Female-to-Male Earnings Ratio, Selected East Asian and Pacific Economies Highlighted**

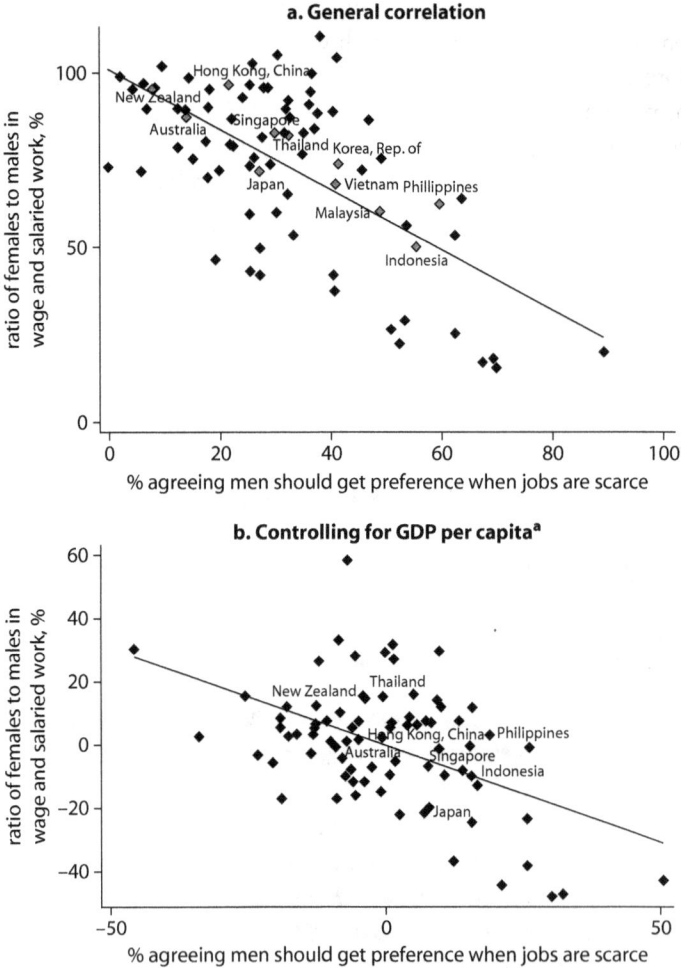

**a. General correlation**

**b. Controlling for GDP per capita[a]**

*Sources:* World Values Survey, latest available data, 1981–2008, http://www.worldvaluessurvey.org/; International Labour Organization Key Indicators of the Labour Market, latest available data, 1981–2008.
*Note:* X-axis displays the percentage of respondents in each economy who agreed with the following statement: "When jobs are scarce, men should have more right to a job than women."
a. GDP = gross national product. coef = −.61070939, se = .12321866, t = −4.96.

gender-based inequality in earnings and participation in relatively secure paid work. This is not a causal statement, as many other variables (such as skills and supply constraints) determine earnings and paid-work participation ratios. The correlation is nevertheless striking and suggests that

**Figure 2.13    Global Correlation of Attitudes toward Female Work and Female-to-Male Earnings Ratio, Selected East Asian and Pacific Economies Highlighted**

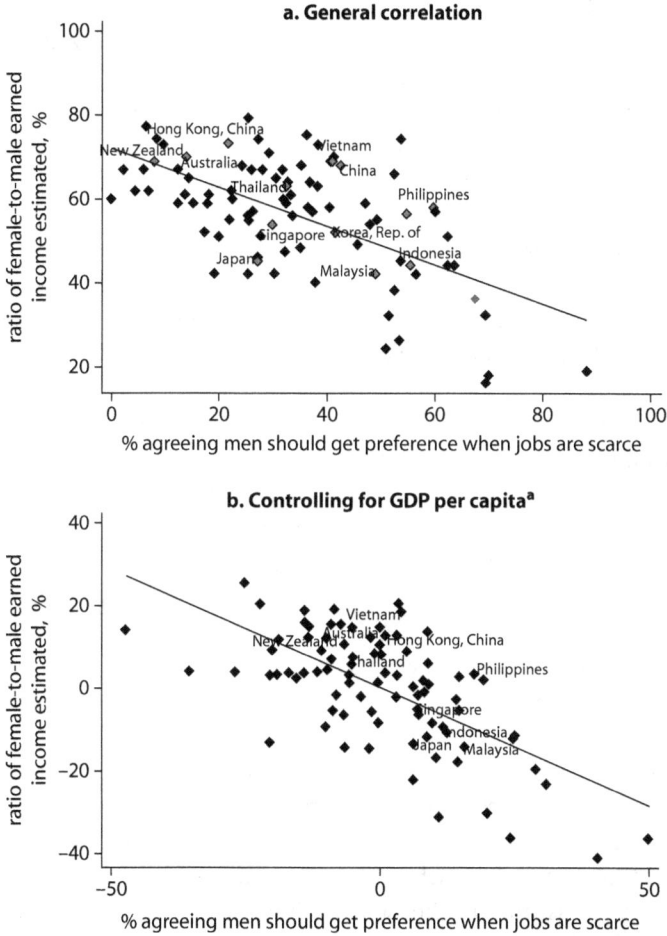

a. General correlation

b. Controlling for GDP per capita[a]

*Sources:* World Values Survey, latest available data, 1981–2008, http://www.worldvaluessurvey.org/; United Nations Development Programme Gender and Development Index, 2008.
*Note:* X-axis displays percentage of respondents in each country who agreed with the following statement: "When jobs are scarce, men should have more right to a job than women."
a. GDP = gross national product. coef = –.56285283, se = .07261313, t = –7.75.

much more research is needed on the relationship between attitudes and economic outcomes for women versus men.

Finally, women's lower business skills may also result from their concentration in the informal sector. Although a large proportion of women in East Asian and Pacific countries are economically "active," a disproportionate share of these women work in the informal sector. Women may be more likely to work in the informal sector because of their larger share of household and family responsibilities; informal employment often allows them to work from home (Gallaway and Bernasek 2002). The informal labor market may also offer a last resort for many women for whom other inequalities, such as in education and vocational training opportunities, mean they cannot find work in the formal sector (UNESCAP 2007). Where women are confined to low-skilled jobs in the informal sector, they are unlikely to gain access to opportunities for business skills development. Moreover, traditional ideas about the jobs most suited to women (for example, service sector jobs in nursing, child care, and community-based work), while hugely valuable, are not always consistent with business skill development.

*Time poverty.* Time is one of the most important assets needed to set up and sustain a successful enterprise, especially in many developing countries, where the process of setting up a business and the day-to-day dealings with bureaucracy are often extremely time consuming. A strong body of evidence from other developing regions indicates that women are more "time poor" than men (see Kes and Swaminathan 2006 for data on gender and time poverty in Sub-Saharan Africa). Women's role as children's caregivers, too, leaves them less time to devote to their economically productive roles, to deal with complex and cumbersome regulations, and to negotiate with government officials.

Although systematic time poverty data—of the kind available for other LDC regions—is difficult to come by for the East Asian and Pacific countries in question, evidence suggests that women in the region do face unequal time pressure. In China, for example, women spend about twice as much time as men on household chores (ADB 2006a). In Vietnam, women's disproportionate share of household work means their working days are six to eight hours longer than men's (ADB 2002). A participatory poverty assessment in Cambodia found, similarly, that women have a wider range of both domestic and nondomestic roles than men; they also wake up earlier and go to sleep later than men do, shouldering as much as 90 percent of the household work, including care of dependents and the sick (ADB 2001). In Mongolia, women have seen an increase in the burden of child care and, consequently, an increase in their time poverty, as government cutbacks caused the number of preschools and kindergartens to decrease by half between 1989 and 1998 (ADB and World Bank 2005). The consequences of time poverty are highlighted by a government survey

of participants in the informal economy of the Philippines, which identified the need to combine economic activity with family responsibilities as
a main reason that women operate in the informal economy (ADB and
World Bank 2008).

A primary reason for women's relative time poverty is their disproportionate responsibility for child rearing. Therefore, a significant factor
determining the level of time poverty that women face is their access to
affordable child care. The EIU developed a five-point scale to indicate the
availability, affordability, and quality of child care services, as well as the
willingness of the extended family to provide child care. A score of 1 represents the lowest access to child care based on these measures, while a
score of 5 represents the greatest level of access. The results in figure 2.14
show that child care appears to be most affordable and widely and easily
available in Australia; Hong Kong, China; and Singapore. Most of the
other countries in the region received a score of 4, indicating good access
to child care on at least two of the measures mentioned above. Indonesia
and Japan both scored a 3, suggesting moderately good access to child
care on at least two of these measures. Finally, Malaysia had the lowest

**Figure 2.14    Access to Child Care, Selected East Asian and Pacific Economies**
*EIU 5-point scale*

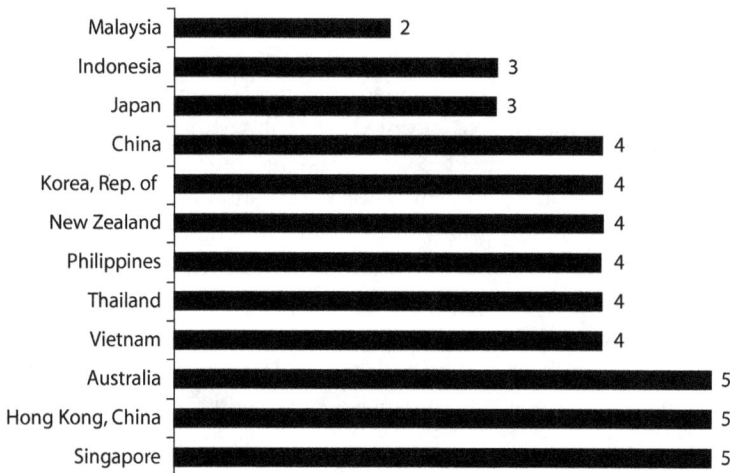

*Source:* EIU, forthcoming.
*Note:* EIU = Economist Intelligence Unit. The figures come from an EIU qualitative analysis (forthcoming) that uses
a five-point scale that indicates the availability, affordability, and quality of child care services, from 1 (lowest) to
5 (highest).

score (2), which indicates that it scores poorly on at least two of the measures outlined above. One country not covered by the index is Mongolia, where, as mentioned above, government cutbacks in social services, including preschools and kindergartens, has increased the child care burden on women (ADB and World Bank 2005).

*Maternity leave benefits.* Maternity leave also influences the extent to which women can balance their reproductive and work roles, as both employers and employees. There are three principal policy issues to consider with respect to maternity leave provisions:

- *Legislated provision for universal coverage:* The legal right to a minimum length of maternity leave and the prohibition of discrimination or dismissal on pregnancy-related grounds along with universal coverage for all employed women
- *Cash benefit:* The provision of a minimum level of income benefits during leave
- *Financing:* A mechanism for financing maternity leave entitlements in a way that minimizes the direct cost impact on employers, as opposed to a financing mandate on employers that creates a disincentive against hiring younger female workers because of the potential additional cost burden

ILO Convention 183, adopted in 2000, stipulates that signatories provide at least 14 weeks of paid leave and that the cash benefit should be equivalent to at least two-thirds of a woman's previous earnings. It recommends that benefits be provided through "compulsory social insurance" or "public funds" (Article 6[8]). Employers are not meant to be individually liable for direct costs unless national law provided for it before adoption of the Convention or if it is subsequently agreed on by government and employer and employee representative organizations.

Figure 2.15 shows the performance of economies on maternity leave provisioning in legal frameworks and employment regulation. The range of maternity leave provisions varies considerably across the region on three dimensions: duration of minimum leave (as legislation provides), amount of maternity benefits, and the financing of benefits (if any), as detailed in table 2.3. Australia is one of the world's few developed countries that lacks legislated paid maternity leave (along with Lesotho, Papua New Guinea, Swaziland, and the United States).[7] On the other end of the scale, Vietnam makes generous provisions for mothers—including 100 percent of wages for days in prenatal care and childbirth; 120 days' paid leave (150 days if

**Figure 2.15    Maternity Leave Provisioning, Selected East Asian and Pacific Economies**

*EIU 100-point scale*

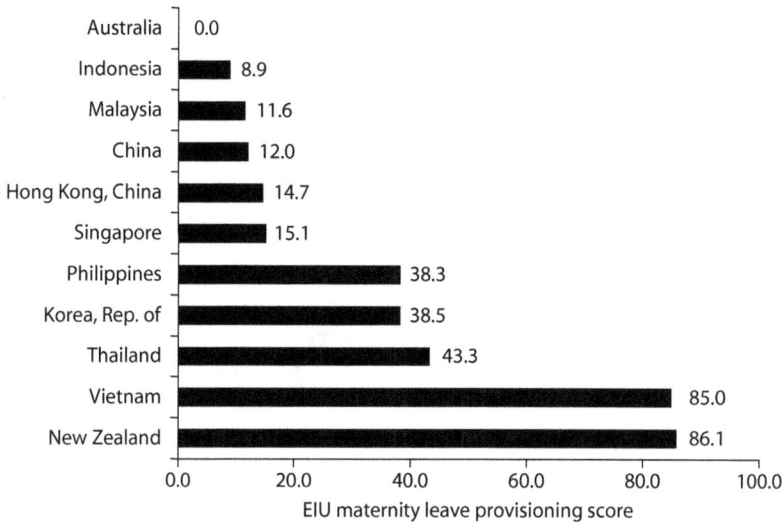

EIU maternity leave provisioning score

*Source:* EIU, forthcoming.

*Note:* EIU = Economist Intelligence Unit. The EIU uses International Labour Organization documents and social security online to create the following scoring code (and then normalizing out of 100). Countries receive 0 for no paid maternity leave (regardless of length of maternity leave); 1 for employer-funded benefits (regardless of length of maternity leave); 2 if they have mixed systems (contributions from both employers and public funds) and less than 14 weeks' maternity leave; 3 for mixed systems (contributions from both employers and public funds) and at least 14 weeks' maternity leave or less than 14 weeks' maternity leave, with maternity leave benefits covered by social insurance or public funds; 4 for at least 14 weeks' maternity leave, with maternity leave benefits covered by social insurance or public funds. Countries score bonus points if they have schemes in place for entrepreneurs; if they have mixed systems for entrepreneurs, an additional 1 point is added to the scoring system above. If they have public funding of maternity leave for entrepreneurs (social insurance or public funds), an additional 2 points are added to the scoring system above. Finally, the following formula was applied: final score multiplied by the percentage of women in the nonagricultural workforce, divided by 100.

in hazardous or arduous employment); and provisions for multiple births, miscarriages, and adoption (U.S. Social Security Administration 2002).

New Zealand recently introduced universal paid maternity leave after listening to the views of employers, women's groups, and the public (World Bank 2010). This provision not only helps to level the playing field for women employees, but also facilitates the employment of women by smaller businesses, which are less able to absorb maternity leave costs on their own. However, it must be added that little research has analyzed the regime that best supports working mothers while also minimizing disincentives for employers to hire women. Indeed, if benefits are overgenerous and

**Table 2.3    Maternity Leave Provisions, East Asian and Pacific Economies as of September 2009**

| Country or area | Length of maternity leave | Quantum of benefit (% of earnings) | Benefit provider |
|---|---|---|---|
| Australia[a] | 52 weeks | No cash benefit | Not applicable |
| Cambodia | 90 days | 50 | Employer |
| China | 90 days | 100 | Employer |
| Fiji | 84 days | Flat rate | Employer |
| Hong Kong, China | 10 weeks | 80 | Employer |
| Indonesia | 3 months | 100 | Employer |
| Korea, Rep. of | 90 days | 100 | Employer for 60 days, employment insurance fund for 30 days |
| Lao PDR | 90 days | 100 | Social security or employer |
| Malaysia | 60 days | 100 | Employer |
| Mongolia | 120 days | 70 | Social insurance fund |
| New Zealand | 14 weeks | 100 (up to a ceiling) | State funds (universal and social assistance system) |
| Papua New Guinea | 6+ weeks | | Not available |
| Philippines | 60 days | 100 | Employer (reimbursed by the social security system) |
| Singapore | 16 weeks | 100 | Employer for first 8 weeks, government for last 8 weeks up to a ceiling; for third and subsequent births, government funding for full 16 weeks up to a ceiling |
| Thailand | 90 days | 100, 50 | Employer for 45 days at 100%, social insurance for 90 days at 50% |
| Vanuatu | 12 weeks | 50 | Employer |
| Vietnam | 4–6 months | 100 | Social insurance fund |

*Sources:* U.S. Social Security Administration, http://www.ssa.gov/policy/data_sub50.html); International Labour Organization Maternity Protection Database, http://www.ilo.org/public/english/protection/condtrav/database/index.htm, last updated 2006.

employers are mandated to cover these benefits in their entirety, many reproductive-age women could face exclusion from, or discrimination in, the labor market.

China has made some progress in introducing maternity provisioning through "maternity insurance," which combines 90 days of paid leave with the cost of delivery. Premiums are paid by the participating employers and should not be more than 1 percent of the total wage bill. Individual employees do not pay premiums. While it is encouraging that some statutory provision has been made for working mothers, a serious challenge is adequacy; maternity insurance payments have not kept up with the rising cost of deliveries, with women making large out-of-pocket payments for quality obstetric care (ADB 2006a).

Benefit levels vary in other countries, too, from a rate close to unemployment benefits (for example, in New Zealand) to full wage compensation (for example, in Thailand for the first 45 days of leave and in Vietnam for the full duration of leave). Notably, only two countries in the region—Mongolia and Vietnam—provide at least 14 weeks of leave, with at least two-thirds of previous earnings as compensation per the ILO Convention 183 stipulation (Öun and Trujillo 2005).

It must also be noted that maternity leave provisions usually cover only full-time formal sector workers, implicitly excluding vast numbers of women who operate informally or who undertake casual or part-time work. Moreover, statutes sometimes explicitly exclude certain groups of women. In Korea and the Philippines, for example, the law excludes women who work in family undertakings. In the Philippines and Singapore, certain categories of managers and business executives are also excluded from paid maternity leave provisions (Öun and Trujillo 2005). This latter exclusion is significant because it might constrain the family decisions of executives or impede their career development if taking unpaid maternity leave means they must resign or take a career break. Although research on the impact of exclusions is not available, these are high-priority concerns in terms of both fairness to women executives and the productivity of the affected enterprise.

*Cultural norms.* In general, whether because of family responsibilities or pervasive cultural norms, women tend to have both less time and fewer opportunities than men to engage in business development. Time constraints, for example, make it harder for women to attend trade fairs and make new contacts (ADB and World Bank 2008). Cultural norms in the region also make certain kinds of informal networking more difficult for women. In a World Bank case study, Indonesian businesswoman Layli Maulidya said, for example, that entertaining buyers is "an awkward task for Indonesian women" (see Chapter 3 of this volume, box 3.1).

In many East Asian and Pacific cultures, women may have to take a stand to depart from the usual way of doing business, such as the late-night drinking sessions that are the favored settings for Korean businessmen to make business deals. Data are not yet available to document, in a quantifiable way, these "soft" cultural barriers to women's participation in networking and business development. Anecdotal insights, however, suggest that these soft cultural barriers do play a role in constraining equal economic opportunities for women.

## Opportunities to Learn and Reform: Improving Security and Equality of Access to Assets

As the above discussion makes clear, secure and equitable access to assets—human, financial, technical—is a crucial prerequisite for successful enterprise formation. Getting a preliminary sense of the most binding constraints to women's access to assets could help policy makers to prioritize and sequence the interventions strategically.

With few exceptions, formal legal systems in the East Asia and Pacific region appear to be largely gender neutral, at least concerning ownership laws, albeit with some serious gender gaps in transfer and inheritance rights. Although legal reform is important to ensure that all statutes are gender equal (as well as to ensure proper circumscription of customary law and its relationship to formal constitutional and international commitments—for example, under CEDAW), the real bullets reformers must bite are implementation reforms and head-on challenges to discriminatory customs.

Policy makers in the region could consider the following recommendations to address formal and customary inequities in access to assets:

- Amend inheritance and matrimonial laws to allow women to own, transfer, and use land as collateral. Several countries have taken steps in this regard—for example, recently in the Philippines. Reform momentum must be sustained, particularly by educating both women and service providers about women's rights. A related measure would be promotion of, and education about, joint titling—for example, as Vietnam initiated by creating space for two names on land registration certificates.
- Improve the environment for, and access to, targeted vocational and business training to nurture the human capital of budding women entrepreneurs. In addition, improve women's on-the-job training prospects by, among other reforms, equalizing retirement ages and providing fiscal and other incentives for enterprises to provide training to women employees.

- Improve women's access to traditional finance in addition to micro-finance by increasing banking coverage, credit bureau coverage, and creating customized credit products for women (as done in the Philippines).
- Reduce the pressures on women navigating the trade-off between their reproductive and economically productive roles through, for example, universal provisioning of maternity leave (as in New Zealand) and by increasing coverage and affordability of child care services.

## Notes

1. Figures measure the percentage of SMEs that have bank loans.
2. See "Women in Business" section of DFCU Web site at http://www.dfcu group.com/index.php?option=com_content&task=blogcategory&id=36 &Itemid=152.
3. For Convention 100, a country receives 2 points if the ILO "Notes with satisfaction" each step the country has taken to enforce the terms of the Convention. A country receives 1 point if the ILO "Notes, Notes with interest, Welcomes, or Looks forward to" each step the country has taken to enforce the terms of the Convention. A country receives 0 points if the ILO "Notes with concern, Regrets, Urges, Asks, Reminds, Reiterates, Repeats the request, Requests, Drew attention to" each of the following issues: "Government policy and organisation/committee to promote convention principles"; "Principle of equality in remuneration in practice"; "Principle of equal values in practice"; "Job appraisal/evaluation mechanisms"; "Cooperation with workers and employers' organisations to involve them in achieving wage equality"; and "Law inspection/enforcement mechanisms." For Convention 111, the scoring tracks whether countries have established government policy and organizations or committees aimed at achieving equality and promoting convention principles; acted to ensure that the principles of the convention are domesticated in labor or other laws; made legal provisions against sexual harassment; cooperated with workers and employers' organizations to promote and accept principles of the convention; and created inspection and enforcement mechanisms.
4. To gain the EOCFW citation, despite the lack of a legislated paid maternity leave requirement for the private sector in Australia, employers must offer a minimum of six weeks' paid maternity leave after 12 months of service; allow female managers to work part time; ensure that the percentage of female managers is greater than or equal to 28 percent of the industry average; and undertake an internal pay-equity analysis (if gaps are found, they should be less than the industry average).

5. For more information on HREOC's work on combating sex discrimination, see http://www.hreoc.gov.au/sex_discrimination/index.html.

6. Vocational and technical education is defined as education mainly designed to lead participants to acquire the practical skills, know-how, and understanding necessary for employment in a particular occupation or trade (or class of occupations or trades). Successful completion of such programs normally leads to a labor-market–relevant vocational qualification recognized by the competent authorities (for example, Ministry of Education or employers' associations) in the country in which it is obtained.

7. The Australian government elected in November 2008 approved legislation that will introduce a paid parental leave scheme in 2011, which will provide parents who meet certain criteria with up to 18 weeks' leave at the minimum wage. The scheme will be funded by the state.

8. As noted above, Australia will introduce paid parental leave from 2011. Currently, however, there is no cash benefit for maternity leave.

## References

ADB (Asian Development Bank). 1998. "Women in Thailand: Briefing Paper." ADB, Manila. http://www.adb.org/Documents/Books/Country_Briefing _Papers/Women_in_Thailand/default.asp?p=gender.

———. 2001. "Participatory Poverty Assessment: Cambodia." ADB, Manila. http://www.adb.org/Documents/Books/Participatory_Poverty/Participatory _Poverty.pdf.

———. 2002. "Women in Vietnam: Country Briefing Paper." ADB, Manila. http://www.adb.org/Documents/Books/Country_Briefing_Papers/Women_in _VietNam/women_vie.pdf.

———. 2004. "Country Gender Assessment: Cambodia." ADB, Manila. http:// www.adb.org/Documents/Reports/Country-Gender-Assessments/cga-cam.pdf.

———. 2005. "Country Gender Assessment: Timor-Leste." ADB, Manila. http:// www.adb.org/Documents/Reports/Country-Gender-Assessments/cga-timor- leste.pdf.

———. 2006a. "Country Gender Assessment: China." ADB, Manila. http:// www.adb.org/Documents/Reports/Country-Gender-Assessments/cga-prc.pdf.

———. 2006b. "Country Gender Assessment: Indonesia." ADB, Manila. http://www.adb.org/Documents/Reports/Country-Gender-Assessments/cga- ino.pdf.

———. 2006c. "Country Gender Assessment: Papua New Guinea." ADB, Manila. http://www.adb.org/Documents/Reports/Country-Gender-Assessments/cga- png.pdf.

ADB (Asian Development Bank) and World Bank. 2005. "Joint Country Gender Assessment: Mongolia."ADB, Manila. http://www.adb.org/Documents/Reports/Country-Gender-Assessments/cga-mon.pdf.

———. 2008. "Joint Country Gender Assessment: Philippines." ADB, Manila. http://www.adb.org/Documents/Reports/Country-Gender-Assessments/phi-2008.asp.

Agarwal, Bina. 1994. *A Field of One's Own: Gender and Land Rights in South Asia.* Cambridge, UK: Cambridge University Press.

Allen, E., N. Langowitz, A. Elam, and M. Dean. 2008. "The Global Entrepreneurship Monitor (GEM) 2007 Report on Women and Entrepreneurship." GEM Special Topic Report. Babson College, Babson Park, MA; and London (UK) Business School: GEM. http://www.gemconsortium.org/download/1256240282234/GEM%20GLOBAL%20Womens%20Report%202007.pdf.

ASEP/JDS. World Values Survey Official Data File 1981–2008. v.3. aggregate file producer ASEP/JDS, Madrid.

Ayyagari, M., T. Beck, and A. Demirgüç-Kunt. 2003. "Small and Medium Enterprises across the Globe: A New Database." Policy Research Working Paper WPS3127, World Bank, Washington, DC. http://siteresources.worldbank.org/DEC/Resources/84797-1114437274304/SME_globe.pdf.

Beck, T., L. Laeven, and V. Maksimovic. 2004. "The Determinants of Financing Obstacles." Policy Research Working Paper Series 3204, World Bank, Washington, DC. http://www-wds.worldbank.org/servlet/WDSContentServer/WDSP/IB/2004/02/18/000160016_20040218131618/Rendered/PDF/wps3204.pdf

EIU (Economist Intelligence Unit). Forthcoming. "Women's Economic Opportunity Index." Draft report, EIU, London.

Gallaway, J. H., and A. Bernasek. 2002. "Gender and Informal Sector Employment in Indonesia." *Journal of Economic Issues* 36 (2): 313–21.

Gochoco-Baustista, M. 2009. "Asset Booms and Macroeconomic Outcomes." *Asia-Pacific Social Science Review* 9 (1): 25–34.

Greater London Authority. 2007. *Women in London's Economy.* London: Greater London Authority. http://www.london.gov.uk/mayor/economic_unit/docs/womenlondoneconomy2007.pdf.

Han, V., and R. Baumgarte. 2000. "Economic Reform, Private Sector Development, and the Business Environment in Viet Nam." *Comparative Economic Studies,* 42 (3): 1–30.

IFC (International Finance Corporation). 2003. "Pacific Enterprise Development Facility SME Business Survey." PowerPoint presentation delivered at IFC meetings in Fiji and in Sydney, Australia.

———. 2006a. "Voices of Women in the Private Sector (Indonesia)." Report for the IFC and the Mekong Private Sector Development Facility, IFC,

Washington, DC. http://www.ifc.org/ifcext/sustainability.nsf/AttachmentsBy
Title/p_Gender_IndonesiaVoices/$FILE/Indonesia+Voices_full_english
.pdf.

———. 2006b. "Voices of Vietnamese Women Entrepreneurs." Report for the IFC,
the Mekong Private Sector Development Facility, and the Gender
Entrepreneurship Markets initiative, IFC, Washington, DC. http://www.ifc
.org/ifcext/mekongpsdf.nsf/AttachmentsByTitle/Voice+of+Women+Entrepr
eneurs-Eng/$FILE/Voice+of+Women+Entrepreneurs+en.pdf.

———. 2006c. "Women Business Owners in Vietnam: A National Survey." Private
Sector Discussions Paper 21 for the Mekong Private Sector Development
Facility and the IFC's Gender Entrepreneurship Markets Initiative, IFC,
Washington, DC. http://www.ifc.org/ifcext/sustainability.nsf/AttachmentsBy
Title/art_GEMTools_MPDF-IFCGEMSurvey/$FILE/WBO+VN+survey+
en.pdf.

———. n.d. "IFC Quick Note: Gender Equal Land Laws; Driving Businesses
Forward." Online brief, IFC, Washington, DC. http://www.ifc.org/ifcext/
enviro.nsf/AttachmentsByTitle/art_GEMquicknote_LandLaws/$FILE/art_Q
uickNotes_LandLaws.pdf.

Kaufmann, Daniel, Geeta Batra, and Andrew H. W. Stone. 2003. "The Firms
Speak: What the World Business Environment Survey Tells Us about
Constraints on Private Sector Development." Paper 8213, University Library
of Munich. http://ideas.repec.org/p/pra/mprapa/8213.html.

Kantor, P. 2001. "Promoting Women's Entrepreneurship Development Based on
Good Practice Programmes: Some Experiences from the North to the South."
Report for ILO InFocus Programme on Boosting Employment through Small
Enterprise Development (IFP/SEED) Working Paper 9, International Labour
Organization, Geneva. http://www.economia.gob.mx/pics/p/p2760/cipi_1D
Promoviendo_desarrollo_mujeres_empresariasOIT.pdf.

Kes, A., and H. Swaminathan. 2006. "Gender and Time Poverty in Sub-Saharan
Africa." In *Gender, Time Use and Poverty in Sub-Saharan Africa*, ed. Mark
Blackden and Quentin Wodon, 13–26. Washington, DC: World Bank.

Land Tenure Center. 2003. "Joint Titling in Nicaragua, Indonesia and Honduras:
Rapid Appraisal Synthesis." Research paper, Land Tenure Center, University of
Wisconsin-Madison. http://minds.wisconsin.edu/bitstream/handle/1793/
22043/89_sl0301joi.pdf?sequence=1.

Li, Huiying, et al. 2002. *Gender and Public Policy*. Beijing: Contemporary China
Publishing House.

New Zealand Pacific Business Council. 2009. "Tonga Dismisses Criticism of
Women's Group on CEDAW." News release, October 2. http://www.nzpbc.co
.nz/index.php?option=com_content&view=article&id=472:-tonga-dismisses-
criticism-of-womens-group-on-cedaw-&catid=8:tonga-news&Itemid=39.

OECD (Organisation for Economic Co-operation and Development). 2003. "Corporate Governance in Asia: A Comparative Perspective." White paper, OECD, Paris. http://www.oecd.org/dataoecd/4/12/2956774.pdf

Öun, I., and Gloria Pardo Trujillo. 2005. *Maternity at Work: A Review of National Legislation; Findings from the ILO's Conditions of Work and Employment Database.* Geneva: International Labour Organization.

Pham, Hoa Thi Mong. 2008. "The Facts about Women's Retirement Age in Vietnam." *World Bank Group Gender Action Plan Newsletter.* Fall edition. http://siteresources.worldbank.org/INTGENDER/Images/336002-1205956505684/gnewsletterp8.pdf.

Sabharwal, G., and T. Huong. 2007. "Differential Retirement Age: Another Face to Gender Discrimination." Brief. Brighton, UK: Eldis document store. http://www.eldis.org/vfile/upload/1/document/0710/Differential%20Retirement%20Age.doc.

Seguino, Stephanie. 2000. "Accounting for Asian Economic Growth." *Feminist Economics* 6 (3): 27–58.

Sheng, Andrew. 2003. "The Future of Capital Markets in East Asia: Implications for China's Equity Markets." Working Paper 192, Stanford Center for International Development, Stanford University, Stanford, CA. http://www.stanford.edu/group/siepr/cgi-bin/siepr/?q=system/files/shared/pubs/papers/pdf/credpr192.pdf.

Siliphong, Phothong, Outhaki Khampoui, and Zuki Mihyo. 2005. "Lao PDR Gender Profile." Working paper 45572, World Bank, Washington, DC. http://siteresources.worldbank.org/INTLAOPRD/Resources/Lao-Gender-Report-2005.pdf.

UNESCAP (United Nations Economic and Social Commission for Asia and the Pacific). 2007. "Economic and Social Survey of Asia and the Pacific 2007." Annual report, UNESCAP, Bangkok.

U.S. Social Security Administration (SSA). 2002. "Social Security Programs throughout the Asia Pacific Region: Vietnam." Online report, SSA, Washington, DC. http://www.ssa.gov/policy/docs/progdesc/ssptw/2002-2003/asia/vietnam.html.

Wanyeki, L.M., ed. 2003. *Women and Land in Africa: Culture, Religion and Realizing Women's Rights.* London: Zed Books.

Weeks, Julie, and Duc D. Dang. 2006. "Targeted Policies that Support Women's Entrepreneurship Can Boost Vietnam's Economic Growth." Briefing Paper, World Bank, Washington, DC.

World Bank. 2002. "Land-use Rights and Gender Equality in Vietnam." *Promising Approaches to Engendering Development* 1 (September): 1. World Bank, Washington, DC. http://siteresources.worldbank.org/INTGENDER/Resources/september2002number1.pdf.

————. 2006a. "China—Governance, Investment Climate, and Harmonious Society: Competitiveness Enhancement for 120 Cities in China." Investment Climate Assessment, World Bank, Washington, DC.

————. 2006b. "Indonesia Country Gender Assessment." World Bank, Washington, DC.

————. 2006c. "Vietnam: Country Gender Assessment." World Bank, Washington, DC.

————. 2007a. "China—Micro and Small Enterprise Finance Project." Project appraisal document, World Bank, Washington, DC.

————. 2007b. "Lao—Private Sector and Investment Climate Assessment: Reducing Investment Climate Constraints to Higher Growth." Investment Climate Assessment, World Bank, Washington, DC.

————. 2007c. "Mongolia—Promoting Investment and Job Creation: An Investment Climate Assessment and Trade Integration Study." Investment Climate Assessment, World Bank, Washington, DC.

————. 2008. *Doing Business 2009*. Washington, DC: World Bank.

————. 2009. *Doing Business 2010*. Washington, DC: World Bank.

————. 2010. *"Economic Opportunities for Women in East Asia and the Pacific Region."* Washington, DC: World Bank.

————. *EdStats*. http://go.worldbank.org/ITABCOGIV1

————. n.d. *Doing Business* Gender Law Library database, World Bank, Washington, DC.

World Values Survey Association. 2009. World Values Survey 1981–2008 official aggregate v.20090901. World Values Survey association. aggregate file producer: ASEP/JDS, Madrid. http://www.worldvaluessurvey.org.

# CHAPTER 3

# Starting a Business

The legal and regulatory framework can have a significant impact on the speed, efficiency, and cost of starting an enterprise and formally registering it. World Bank case studies of female entrepreneurs in the East Asia and Pacific region indicate that female entrepreneurs' success at negotiating this environment can be an important factor in determining their entrepreneurial success (World Bank 2010).

Global evidence confirms this finding. Research suggests that ease of business entry (as measured by the number of actions and time required to complete entry formalities) is correlated with number of enterprises, particularly in the SME sector where many women operate. Conversely, the costs of entry-regulation procedures across countries correlate negatively to the percentage of new firms in an industry (Klapper, Laeven, and Rajan 2006). For example, figure 3.1 shows the negative correlation between the number of entry procedures and business entry rates.

While entrepreneurs consider many other factors (for example, tax regimes and operational regulations) before deciding to formalize their businesses, the evidence clearly points to the cost and number of entry procedures as one important determinant of this decision.

Table 3.1 shows the performance of the East Asian and Pacific region on the ease of starting a business relative to other regions. The region

**Figure 3.1    Global Correlation of Start-Up Procedures and Business Entry Rates, Selected Countries**

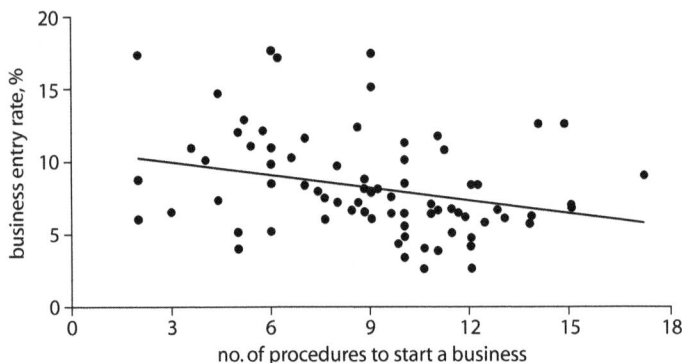

*Sources:* World Bank Enterpreneurship Database, 2007; World Bank 2003, 2004, 2005, 2006a.

**Table 3.1    Requirements to Start a Business, by Region**

| Region or economy | Procedures (number) | Duration (days) | Cost (% GNI per capita) | Minimum capital (% of income per capita) |
|---|---|---|---|---|
| OECD[a] | 5.7 | 13 | 4.7 | 15.5 |
| East Asia and the Pacific | 8.1 | 41 | 25.8 | 21.3 |
| Eastern Europe and Central Asia | 6.7 | 17.4 | 8.3 | 21.5 |
| Latin America and the Caribbean | 9.5 | 61.7 | 36.6 | 2.9 |
| Middle East and North Africa | 7.9 | 20.7 | 34.1 | 129.7 |
| South Asia | 7.3 | 28.1 | 27 | 26.9 |
| Sub-Saharan Africa | 9.4 | 45.6 | 99.7 | 144.7 |

*Source:* World Bank 2009.
*Note:* GNI = gross national income; OECD = Organisation for Economic Co-operation and Development.
a. See table 2.1, c.

performs poorly compared to Organisation for Economic Co-operation and Development (OECD) countries and about average relative to the other geographic regions. However, the number of procedures and the cost (as a percentage of gross national income [GNI]) is quite high, both absolutely and relatively.

The region shows significant cross-country variation on these indicators, as shown in figure 3.2, which compares the number of days and procedures required to start up a business. The huge variation ranges from

**Figure 3.2    Number of Days and Procedures Required to Start a Business, East Asian and Pacific Economies**

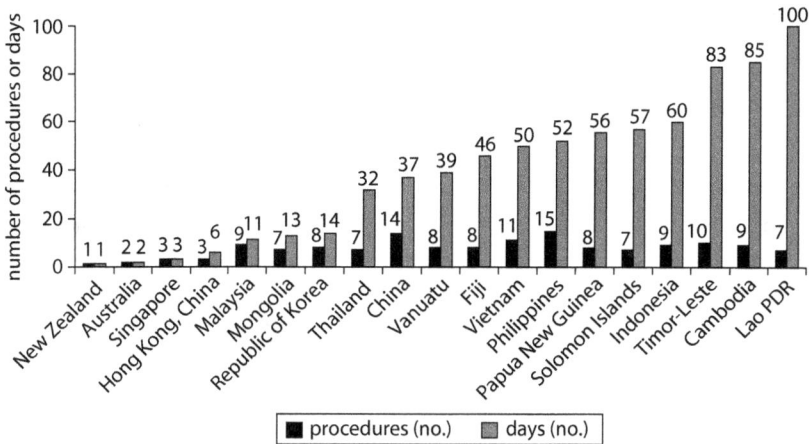

*Source:* World Bank 2009.

the rather short start-up times required in places such as Malaysia, New Zealand, and Singapore to the long delays aspiring entrepreneurs must tolerate in Cambodia, Lao PDR, and Timor-Leste, for example.

The time burden imposed on prospective entrepreneurs arises from the number, complexity, and cost of entry regulations; the impact of multiple layers of regulations at different levels of government; and the endogenous interaction between informality and small size on the one hand and regulatory burden on the other. This chapter discusses these specific regulatory issues before turning to an analysis of other salient general business environment factors, including corruption, enforcement of contracts, and the way in which decentralization and other political processes might affect women's "voice" in public-private dialogue to shape the environment for their enterprises.

## Entry Regulations

Numerous and lengthy procedures, as well as high monetary costs, often prevent potential entrepreneurs from even starting their businesses, or at least from registering them formally. In principle, one might expect the regulatory environment to affect male- and female-led enterprises in the same way. However, anecdotal evidence (see boxes 2.1 and 3.1) suggests

**Box 3.1**

## Case Study Excerpt

### Indonesia: Layli Maulidya
Partner, CV Karya Wahana Sentosa

Layli Maulidya stands out as one of the few women running a business in Indonesia's furniture industry. However, it has not been an easy ride. To register a business as a limited liability company in Indonesia requires minimum start-up capital equal to 74 percent of the average national income. "Starting up as a limited liability company is not a real option open to many potential entrepreneurs," Maulidya says. "If you can afford an agent, it is much simpler. [However] paying additional fees to hire an agent to help you through the process is a luxury not many start-up entrepreneurs can afford."

The complexity and costs associated with registering a business prevented Maulidya from registering as a limited liability business, which meant she could not take advantage of the risk-optimizing possibilities available through the limited liability business structure. Instead, she registered the business as a less-advantageous private partnership (CV). "In the event of any third-party claims against the CV, the shareholder's personal assets can be seized in order to pay the company's liabilities," Maulidya explains. Conversely, the court system also seems stacked against smaller Indonesian businesses, she notes. "Given the length of time that we have to spend in court and the money we have to spend on attorney fees, recovering overdue debts through the court system would cost more than the amount that we wanted to claim," she says.

If the costs and complexity of the process were reduced, more women could register limited liability businesses, benefiting not only the women business owners, but also the government. As Maulidya points out, "More registered businesses means higher revenues for the government."

*Source:* World Bank 2010.

that the regulatory environment assumes a gendered dimension because women tend to have less access than men to social networks to help them navigate patronage-based bureaucracies; have access to less and poorer-quality information; and, crucially, have less time to negotiate complex procedures. Research on the differential regulatory burden faced by female and male entrepreneurs would be useful in understanding which procedures impose particular costs on women—and how best to mitigate those costs.

In the region, Cambodia, Indonesia, the Philippines, and Vietnam have particularly difficult entry regulations. Case studies of female entrepreneurs from these countries confirm this (see box 3.1). Cambodia, for example, ranks the lowest of any East Asian and Pacific country (173/183) under the *Doing Business* "starting a business" indicator (World Bank 2009). Nine procedures are necessary to start a business, and the average time taken for the whole process is 85 days (World Bank 2007a). The monetary cost is also significant. The cost of registering a business in Cambodia equates to a high 138.4 percent of the average national income. The case-study excerpt in box 3.1 highlights the impact of the costs and complexities of registering a limited liability business in Indonesia. Indonesia, too, has a low *Doing Business* ranking (161/183) for starting a business. To register a business as a limited liability company in Indonesia requires a minimum start-up capital equal to 59.7 percent of the average national income. The case-study excerpt in box 3.1 highlights the impact of the costs and complexities of registering a limited liability business in Indonesia (World Bank 2010).

Vietnam has made some headway at simplifying business entry regulations. With the introduction of simplified procedures, including some e-government processes under the Vietnam Enterprise Law 1999, the number of businesses established in 2000–05 tripled compared to figures for the previous decade (Nguyen and others 2006). However, there are still an estimated 2 million informal household businesses in the country, and Vietnam still ranks relatively low on the *Doing Business 2010* "starting a business" indicator (116 out of 183 economies) (World Bank 2009). Delays arise because of the long periods required to acquire a registration certificate (15 days), obtain a company seal (14 days), register for a tax code, and purchase preprinted invoices (15 days) (Nguyen and others 2006). While applicants can now track some processes online, they still must physically go to the government office to submit their documents (Nguyen and others 2006).

In several countries in the region, the difficulties of starting a business are exacerbated through high minimum capital requirements. In Timor-Leste, for example, capital requirements represent 333.1 percent of per capita GNI. High minimum start-up capital requirements are highlighted as a significant constraint in case-studies of female entrepreneurs in the Republic of Korea and Indonesia (see box 3.1). The Korean businesswoman profiled in a World Bank case study obtained the required capital through access to her family's business resources (World Bank 2010). This is a luxury, as the entrepreneur herself recognizes, and is unlikely to be available to other women entrepreneurs in her country. Encouragingly, the Republic of Korea has now introduced a reform abolishing the minimum paid-up capital requirement altogether. Singapore also offers a good example to the rest of the region, with no minimum capital requirements for starting a business (World Bank 2008).

## The Gender Dimensions of Regulatory Burden and Informality

The costs of starting a business are often higher for women than for men, even when the enterprises they lead face the same regulatory environments, as argued above. As a consequence, women are more likely to operate informally. Informality, in turn, reduces the probability of obtaining credit and the ability of a business to enforce contracts. An excessive regulatory burden thus acts as a disincentive to growth and formalization, while small size and informality further increase the burden of regulatory costs, creating a vicious cycle.

Evidence confirms both sides of the circular link. Countries where there is a smaller SME sector and larger informal sector are also those countries where it is more costly (in monetary terms as well as in terms of the number of procedures) to register a business (Ayyagari, Beck, and Demirgüç-Kunt 2003). This finding is echoed in the World Business Environment Survey, which indicates that smaller firms are more likely than larger firms to face significant barriers to doing business (Batra, Kaufmann, and Stone 2003). For example, the ADB Country Gender Assessment for the Philippines finds that microenterprises generally have little or no margins to survive bureaucratic delays (ADB and World Bank 2008). The Lao PDR Investment Climate Assessment echoes this finding, adding that high fixed and sunk costs associated with clearing regulatory hurdles have prevented or discouraged many firms from registering as formal businesses (World Bank 2007c).

Many women in the informal sector operate as small-scale entrepreneurs and display remarkable ingenuity and creativity in sustaining their livelihoods. However, the negative impact that informality has on businesses' access to credit and their ability to enforce contracts makes it difficult for women to develop and expand their businesses. The problems associated with informality have become more critical in recent years with the burgeoning of the informal sector in many countries.

A World Bank study found that rapid rural-urban migration and the consequent surge in population in Asian cities has not been managed effectively, leading to a substantial increase in inequality and an increase in the size of the informal labor market (Gill and others 2007). In China, the informal labor market has been estimated to represent 40 percent of its total labor market (Gill and others 2007). In the Philippines, the figure is even higher, at 49 percent (ADB and World Bank 2008). In Lao PDR, the informal economy contributes around 30 percent of GDP (World Bank 2007c).

Finally, given the current economic climate, the importance of the informal sector is likely to increase further, as evidence has linked economic crises with growth of the informal sector (Horn 2009). After the 1997 financial crisis, for example, Indonesia saw an increase in informal sector workers from 65 percent in 1998 to 71 percent in 2003 (World Bank 2006b). Given the depth and severity of the current financial and economic crisis, it is possible that we may see further shifts toward informal work. This is likely to hit women entrepreneurs and workers hard due to their particular vulnerabilities (see box 3.2).

**Box 3.2**

## Economic Crisis, Informality, and the Vulnerability of Women

Although the full details of the effects of the 2008–09 financial and economic crisis will not be fully understood for a while yet, various analyses have pointed out that women are a key vulnerable group who may be disproportionately affected (ILO 2009; ADB 2009; UNESCAP 2009). Women as workers are concentrated in sectors that are particularly hard hit: export-oriented manufacturing, agricultural exports, mining, and tourism. Moreover, women tend to be concentrated in nonregular and informal forms of employment, and evidence shows that such nonregular workers—casual, contract, temporary, or seasonal—have suffered the most from the first wave of the job cuts resulting from the crisis (ILO 2009).

An ILO technical note on the gender effects of the crisis substantiates this claim. The note presents data for the sectors most severely affected by the crisis in the Philippines, Thailand, and Vietnam, and shows that women are paid lower wages and are concentrated in nonregular employment and unskilled or semiskilled jobs. Based on emerging trends under the current crisis and the experience of the 1997 Asian crisis, the note shows that these nonregular, low-paid, and unskilled or semiskilled workers are more likely to be the first to lose their jobs (ILO 2009).

The crisis will also affect female entrepreneurs as they are also concentrated in the informal sector—particularly in the most vulnerable forms of informal

*(continued)*

**Box 3.2** *(continued)*

employment (for example, as street vendors) (Horn 2009). Research suggests that during crises, the number of workers in the informal sector rises; this results in increased competition for informal entrepreneurs, who may have to lower prices to stay in business. Indeed, one study in Thailand found that 80 percent of street vendors questioned had reported increased competition since the crisis unfolded. Additionally, informal entrepreneurs do not have a lot of bargaining power and often have no choice but to adjust to changes in the prices of goods bought and sold by middlemen (Horn 2009). Finally, the labor market contraction might push more women into "necessity" entrepreneurship, especially where they are crowded out from their regular positions in the labor market by men who have lost their formal sector jobs (ILO 2009).

## Other Business Environment Issues

Both female and male entrepreneurs face other significant business constraints throughout the region, but these constraints may hit women-led enterprises especially hard. They include corruption and costly and cumbersome legal and regulatory frameworks for trade and exchange (especially for enforcement of contracts). Women also face particular problems with gender-biased enforcement procedures and societal customs (which sometimes even take precedence over statutory laws). Increasing women's level of influence in public-private dialogue at both national and local levels is also necessary to foster inclusive private sector development, growth, and poverty reduction agendas.

### Governance

With some exceptions (for example, Hong Kong, China; and Singapore), entrepreneurs routinely identify corruption as a significant constraint to doing business in the East Asia and Pacific region (Gill and others 2007). Corruption raises the costs of doing business and creates a more unpredictable business environment, making it harder to plan ahead. It may also create an incentive for firms to stay informal, in order to escape the discretionary power of local officials.

Corruption hits women-led enterprises particularly hard because officials with discretionary power can exploit the relatively poorer information that women have about regulations and their entitlement to service standards. This comes out starkly in several case studies of individual female entrepreneurs in the region (World Bank 2010). One such case study, of a group of female entrepreneurs in the Solomon Islands, brings into relief how the arbitrary power of local officials can prevent enterprises from registering and operating formally (see box 3.3).

**Box 3.3**

## Case Study Excerpt

### Solomon Islands: Women for Peace

Westside Women for Peace started with a noble goal: to promote peace among women from different ethnic groups and ensure economic security by selling their wares at a joint marketplace. But legal and administrative obstacles prevented their access to land, forcing the women to operate informally.

Access to land is the most problematic issue for entrepreneurs in the Solomon Islands, which ranks 172 out of 183 economies in the World Bank's *Doing Business 2010* " registering property" indicator (World Bank 2009). In the Solomon Islands, the process of registering property requires 10 procedures, takes up to 297 days, and costs 4.8 percent of property value.

As Westside Women for Peace discovered, this creates opportunities for corruption. After lengthy delays and making a requested payment to a government official in good faith, obtaining a fixed-term lease for market space proved impossible.

Westside Women for Peace decided in 2004 to apply for a fixed-term lease to build a permanent market structure, warehouse, and training center. Transferring property in the Solomon Islands requires the approval of the commissioner of lands (ministerial consent), which is uncommon in most countries. In February 2004, Westside Women for Peace wrote to the commissioner of land to ask for a fixed-term lease. In 2005, they received a response from a high-level government official who said the women should deal directly with him rather than the land commissioner, but that they would need to pay US$570 for the lease to even be considered. The women paid this amount directly to this government official but never heard from him again.

On November 15, 2005, the women received an eviction notice from the government official, informing them that he was now their landlord—an indication that he had purchased the land.

*Source:* World Bank 2010.

Discretionary power, and the propensity to demand side payments, is rife in other countries too. In Cambodia, entrepreneurs consistently report that corruption is a major constraint and that informal charges prevent them from expanding their businesses (World Bank 2007b). Similarly, business climate studies in Indonesia highlighted "illegal levies" as one of the major constraints faced by female entrepreneurs, with almost 50 percent of female-owned businesses citing corruption as a "severe" constraint (IFC 2006; World Bank 2007c). In Mongolia, corruption is the leading concern of firms, with 56 percent of questioned firms rating it as the most significant constraint to doing business (World Bank 2007d).

A contributing factor to corruption in the region is rapid or poorly managed decentralization programs, which give considerable discretion to individual officials to implement and oversee complex laws and procedures (IFC 2006). Surveys of businesses in Indonesia and the Philippines suggest that major decentralization has led to worsening corruption (Gill and others 2007). Vietnam, which has also implemented a program of decentralization, has also experienced problems with corruption; in one province, 70 percent of businesses reported that they had to pay bribes, while 12 percent claimed that more than 10 percent of annual revenue was spent on informal charges (Malesky and others 2008).

Opportunities for corruption are also greater where business regulations are too numerous and overly complex. A case study of a female entrepreneur in Indonesia (see box 3.1) refers to the large number of procedures as the reason for widespread corruption and high costs, as middlemen and officials offer to "speed up" processes in exchange for under-the-table payments (resembling the situation faced by the Solomon Islands businesswomen in box 3.3) (World Bank 2010). Corruption imposes costs for all businesses, but there is some evidence that women find themselves particularly affected because of public officials' perception that they are "soft targets."[1]

### *Enforcement of Contracts*

A well-designed, well-implemented legal framework for trade and exchange (that is, for enforcement of contracts) is, in many senses, at the heart of the quality of the business environment. The costs and difficulties of enforcing contracts can be considerable, particularly for women who are time poor, live far from metropolitan legal centers, are unaware of their legal rights and available recourses, or lack the resources to afford legal expertise. Table 3.2 shows the *Doing Business 2010* figures for the "enforcing contracts" indicator (World Bank 2009). Country performance varies widely: In Singapore, enforcing contracts costs only 26 percent of the claim

**Table 3.2    Contract Enforcement in the East Asia and Pacific Region**

| Economy | Procedures (number) | Time (days) | Cost (% of claim) |
|---|---|---|---|
| Australia | 28 | 395 | 20.7 |
| Cambodia | 44 | 401 | 102.7 |
| China | 34 | 406 | 11.1 |
| Fiji | 34 | 397 | 38.9 |
| Hong Kong, China | 24 | 280 | 19.5 |
| Indonesia | 39 | 570 | 122.7 |
| Lao PDR | 42 | 443 | 31.6 |
| Malaysia | 30 | 585 | 27.5 |
| Mongolia | 32 | 314 | 30.6 |
| New Zealand | 30 | 216 | 22.4 |
| Papua New Guinea | 42 | 591 | 110.3 |
| Philippines | 37 | 842 | 26.0 |
| Singapore | 21 | 150 | 25.8 |
| Solomon Islands | 37 | 455 | 78.9 |
| Thailand | 35 | 479 | 12.3 |
| Timor-Leste | 51 | 1435 | 163.2 |
| Vanuatu | 30 | 430 | 74.7 |
| Vietnam | 34 | 295 | 28.5 |

*Source:* World Bank 2009.

amount and takes an average of 150 days, but in Timor-Leste, the corresponding figures are 163 percent of the claim and a staggering 1,435 days.

Timor-Leste is the most difficult place in the world to enforce contracts, ranking 183rd of 183 economies on this indicator in *Doing Business 2010*. Businesses must grapple with high costs, numerous procedures, and an average wait time of almost five years. A Timorese entrepreneur profiled in a series of case studies (World Bank 2010) confirms that chasing unpaid bills was the major obstacle for her business. Verbal, rather than written, contracts have formed the mainstay of her business in a country where contacts and relationships are the main channels for securing customers. Businesses have little incentive to enter into written contracts because the court system takes too long to process cases and costs a considerable amount in attorney and court fees.

While alternative dispute resolution systems can be both cost-effective and efficient, in Timor-Leste, alternative dispute resolution relies on the intervention of community leaders, and a major gender barrier applies: women are not allowed to join the congregation unless invited by these leaders to discuss disputes. Problems with customary, gender-biased enforcement procedures exist in various forms in other countries. In chapter 2, the section on access to land cited examples when customary procedures sometimes take precedence even over statutory laws.

The costs and difficulties associated with enforcing contracts are also cited as a strong constraint on effective business operations by an Indonesian businesswoman profiled in a World Bank case study (see box 3.1) (World Bank 2010). Recovering a debt in Indonesia can often cost more in attorney fees and court costs than the amount claimed, as *Doing Business 2010* revealed. Indonesia, unsurprisingly, ranks low (146th out of 183 countries) on the *Doing Business* "enforcing contracts" indicator.

### *Public-Private Dialogue and Women's Influence*

In both the public and private sectors, increasing women's participation and voice is necessary for inclusive private sector development, growth, and poverty reduction agendas. At the national level, women are represented to different degrees in all countries in this region, ranging from a high of 32 percent of parliamentarians in New Zealand to a low of 0.9 percent in Papua New Guinea. On a regional level, as figure 3.3 shows, East Asia and the Pacific does not do much better on this score than other developing regions—the Middle East and North Africa, South Asia, and Sub-Saharan Africa—and it does worse than Latin America and the Caribbean.

Although national statistics of women's representation in government are useful, it is also important to look at women's position in local government, especially in the context of decentralization. Evidence to date is mixed. On the one hand, the move to local-level politics can increase the potential for governments to be more accountable to the citizens they are meant to serve and to incorporate local-level concerns (including those of women in different localities) more systematically into their policies. Some evidence suggests that, with decentralization, local governments have started to take women's needs into greater account (for example, in Indonesia [World Bank 2006b] and the Philippines [World Bank 2007e]). On the other hand, more local government power might also have the effect of strengthening discriminatory traditional norms, as identified, for example, in the analysis of Indonesia's decentralization program (World Bank 2006). Moreover, as discussed above, rapid decentralization can sometimes increase corruption, thus harming businesses led by both women and men.

To counter such trends, increased political empowerment and participation for women in all levels of government and in public-private dialogue are critical. The assumption behind this claim is that if women are less involved in public policy, then policy makers are less likely to consider their

**Figure 3.3    Women in Parliament, East Asian and Pacific Countries**

**a. % of seats held by women, by country**

| Country | % |
|---|---|
| New Zealand | 33.1 |
| Timor-Leste | 29.2 |
| Australia | 26.7 |
| Vietnam | 25.8 |
| Lao PDR | 25.2 |
| Singapore | 24.5 |
| China | 21.3 |
| Philippines | 20.5 |
| Cambodia | 16.3 |
| Korea, Rep. of | 13.7 |
| Thailand | 11.7 |
| Indonesia | 11.6 |
| Fiji | 11.3 |
| Malaysia | 10.8 |
| Samoa | 8.2 |
| Mongolia | 4.2 |
| Vanuatu | 3.8 |
| Tonga | 3.1 |
| Papua New Guinea | 0.9 |
| Solomon Islands | 0.0 |

**b. % of seats held by women, by region**

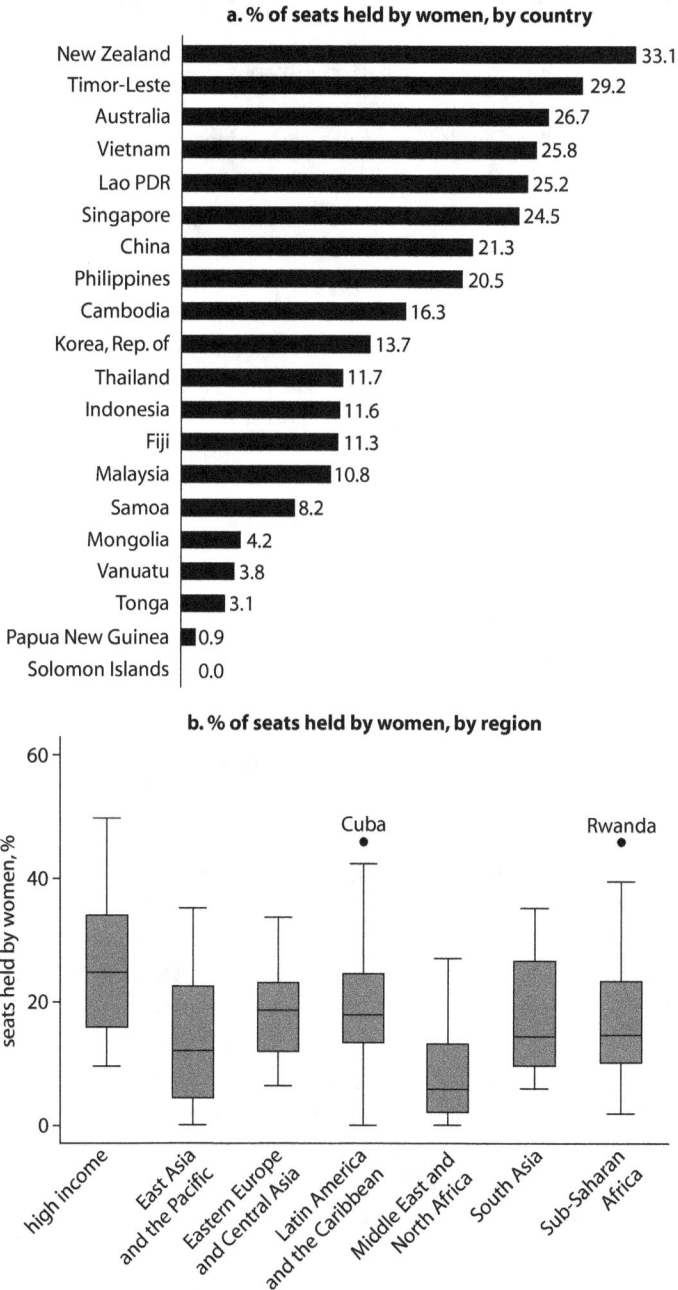

*Source:* World Bank *Gender Stats,* latest available data 1998–2008.
*Note:* For definitions of geographic and high-income regions, see note to figure 2.7.

needs and concerns. In India, a study showed that when leadership positions in village councils were reserved for women, the decisions of those councils would result in greater infrastructure investment that was directly relevant to the needs of rural women (Chattopadhyay and Duflo 2001).

Within the East Asia and Pacific region, another example is that of New Zealand and the evolution of the parliamentary agenda on child care and maternity leave. Between 14.4 percent and 16.5 percent of New Zealand's parliamentary seats were occupied by women from 1987 to 1992. During that time, women politicians were responsible for 50 of the 75 discussions of child care and parental leave. During the next seven years from 1993 to 1999, the same two "women's issues" were mentioned 75 times in the House, with female MPs responsible for 59 of these incidences. During this period, between 21.2 and 29.2 percent of parliamentary seats were held by women (Grey 2001).

Whether "women's issues" get adequate legislative attention is a more complex matter than simply the proportion of women in political decision-making positions, yet the positive correlation is clear. For example, figure 3.4 shows the correlation between the proportion of women in parliament and the Economist Intelligence Unit (EIU) maternity leave score (EIU forthcoming; see figure 2.15 for definition of this score). The significant numbers of data points both above and below the line suggests that more is in play; for example, former socialist countries often make generous maternity leave provisions without significant numbers of women in parliament. However, the correlation remains positive when controlling for GDP per capita.

Although increasing the political participation of women is necessary, it is not sufficient to improve regulatory cognizance of gender issues.[2] On the private sector side, it is important to initiate constructive dialogue between businesspeople and the government officials in charge of private sector development. Evidence is emerging that this sort of public-private dialogue can produce tangible improvements in the business environment, but these improvements must be anchored in credible institutions, have "champions of change" in both government and the private sector, and have high degrees of cooperation *within* the private sector itself. (See, for example, an impact assessment of the effectiveness of public-private dialogue in the Mekong region, which argues that significant reforms in trade facilitation, contract enforcement, and access to land are directly attributable to business forums [HR Inc. and MCG Management Consulting 2008].)

Singapore provides a good example of how public-private dialogue is improving the business environment and helping to ensure that

**Figure 3.4   Global Correlation between Percent of Seats in Parliament Held by Women and Quality of Maternity Leave Provision, East Asian and Pacific Countries Highlighted**

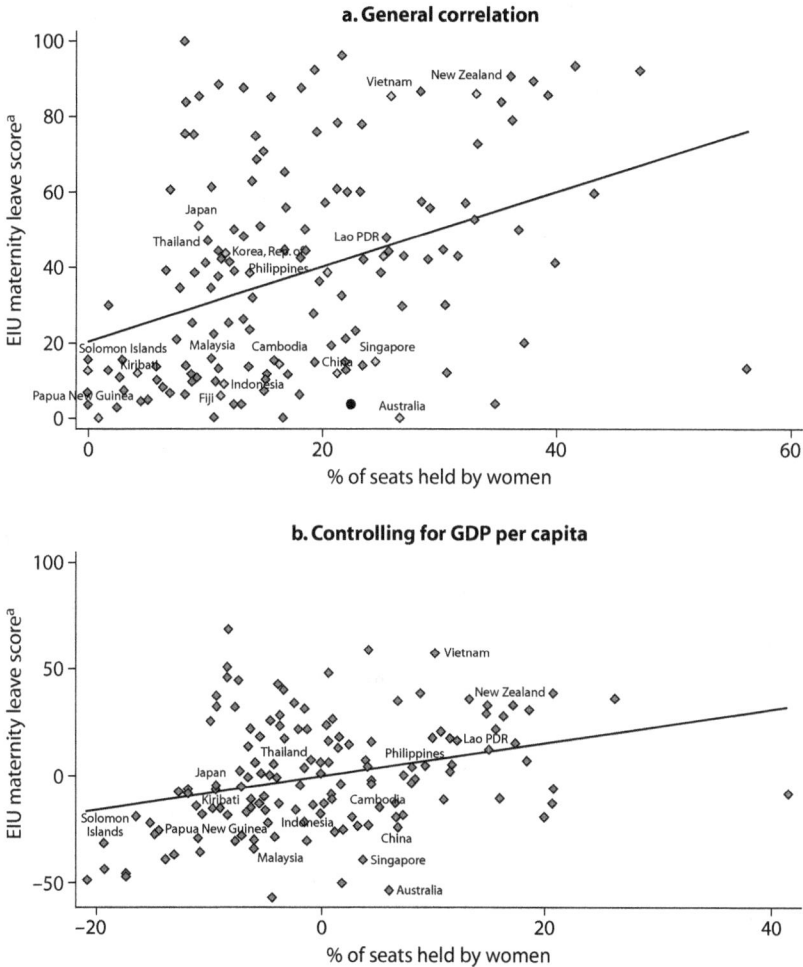

**a. General correlation**

**b. Controlling for GDP per capita**

*Sources:* World Bank Gender Stats, latest available data 2002–08; EIU, forthcoming.
*Note:* GDP = gross national product.
coef = 77581411, se = .20273326, t = 3.83.
a. For definition of EIU maternity leave score and how it is calculated, see note to figure 2.15.

government takes the entrepreneurs' concerns into account when making policy. Singapore's Action Community for Entrepreneurship (ACE) is a public-private collaboration currently led by the minister in charge of entrepreneurship. One of ACE's main objectives is to improve the regulatory environment for businesses by promoting discussion and encouraging feedback from entrepreneurs (World Bank 2010).

The United States provides examples of how coalitions of women business owners have successfully lobbied for fundamental legislative reform. During the 1970s and 1980s, successful lobbying led by the National Association of Women Business Owners led to passage of

- The 1972 Equal Employment Opportunity Act, which prohibited discrimination in hiring based on sex
- The 1974 Equal Credit Opportunity Act, which prohibited discrimination against loan applicants based on sex of applicant and enabled women to get loans and credit cards in their sole names
- The 1988 Women's Business Ownership Act, which eliminated state laws requiring male cosignatories on loans; required the U.S. Census Bureau to accurately count all women-owned businesses; established women's business centers; and created the National Women's Business Council to advise the president, the U.S. Small Business Administration, and Congress on the status of women's enterprise development

In recent years, many other initiatives have been launched to partner with the public sector to ensure more women-friendly business policies. In 1994, the Federal Acquisition Streamlining Act included a target of 5 percent of all federal contracts for women-led business. In 1997, the Women's Business Enterprise National Council was established to help facilitate access to corporate markets for women-owned businesses. Approximately half of all Fortune 500 companies are now committed, as members of the council, to supplier diversity.

Despite this progress, full equality for women in business remains elusive, even in the United States. "Several decades after these initiatives began to level the playing field for women in business, we must admit that women at the highest levels of major American corporations are still quite scarce—just 3 percent of Fortune 500 firms are led by a woman. . . . There is more work to be done," says Marilyn Carlson Nelson, chair of the Carlson Group and 2002–05 chair of the National Women's Business Council (World Bank 2010).

## Opportunities to Learn and Reform: Creating an Enabling Environment for Women-Led Businesses

As the discussion in this chapter makes clear, cumbersome start-up regulations can significantly impede and divert the scarce time of women entrepreneurs. If governments want to capitalize on the growth dividend afforded by vibrant women-led enterprises, they must simplify and reduce the costs of business start-up. Moreover, governments should target support to smaller budding enterprises, accompanied by targeted information campaigns (and incentives) to help women move from the informal sector to formal sector enterprises. The most meaningful concrete steps would include the following:

- Ease minimum capital requirements for business registration.

- Reduce the complexity and number of procedures required for business registration by, for example, creating "one-stop" clearance windows, and further exploring the potential for the greater use of e-government in the registration process, as done in Thailand in recent years.

- Provide incentives to move out of informality through, for example, the targeted promotion of the SME sector. Promoting the SME sector would not only benefit the female entrepreneurs who operate in the sector but also support poverty reduction efforts in developing economies. Research has shown that microenterprises and small enterprises have a positive role to play in poverty reduction as they tend to be less concentrated in urban areas than are larger firms and are more likely to employ poorer people (World Bank 2007a). The Chinese SME promotion model—as a tool against interregional inequality—would be one to explore. Singapore also provides a notable example in its provision of technical and management capacity building through SPRING Singapore (Standards, Productivity, and Innovation Board).

- Systematically and aggressively tackle corruption and the arbitrary power of local officials to stimulate investment and to reduce the costs and risks of going for growth.

- Provide targeted education campaigns about business entry and registration procedures to women entrepreneurs and provide special literacy assistance to women to help them negotiate those procedures.

- Experiment with innovative gender-sensitive social accountability tools and demand-side governance approaches to increase the responsiveness and accountability of local government officials who administer business procedures. In this context, decentralization and deconcentration processes must be managed in a gender-sensitive way by ensuring that localities' increased autonomy does not also increase the sway of discriminatory local norms.

## Notes

1. For example, in Uganda, 43 percent of female entrepreneurs reported harassment from government officials, compared with 25 percent of all entrepreneurs. When reforms simplified business start-up procedures, first-time business owners who were women increased by 33 percent (World Bank 2007a).

2. Indeed, the efficacy of increasing representation to reach "critical mass" depends on the context as well as positional or entrenched power inequalities. As Grey (2001, 15) notes, "Critical mass is a concept that provides an explanation for why women (and other minorities) struggle to impact upon all areas of the political arena. But perhaps what we should talk about is different critical masses—dependent on what we wish to achieve through group representation. Reaching around 15 percent representation in a political body overall allows a voice. It could take a far greater proportion of women throughout the different arms of legislatures to change policy outcomes and the political culture."

## References

ADB (Asian Development Bank). 2009. "Global Economic Crisis: Challenges for Developing Asia and the ADB's Response." ADB, Manila.

ADB (Asian Development Bank) and World Bank. 2008. "Joint Country Gender Assessment: Philippines." ADB, Manila. http://www.adb.org/Documents/Reports/Country-Gender-Assessments/phi-2008.asp.

Ayyagari, M., T. Beck, and A. Demirgüç-Kunt. 2003. "Small and Medium Enterprises across the Globe: A New Database." Policy Research Working Paper WPS3127, World Bank, Washington, DC. http://siteresources.worldbank.org/DEC/Resources/84797-1114437274304/SME_globe.pdf.

Batra, G., D. Kaufmann, and A. Stone. 2003. "The Investment Climate Around the World: Voices of the Firms from the World Business Environment Survey (WBES)." WBES report, World Bank, Washington, DC.

Chattopadhyay, R., and E. Duflo. 2001. "Women as Policy Makers: Evidence from an India-Wide Randomized Policy Experiment." Massachusetts Institute of Technology (MIT) Department of Economics Working Paper 01-35, MIT, Cambridge, MA.

EIU (Economist Intelligence Unit). Forthcoming. "Women's Economic Opportunity Index." Draft report.

Gill, I., H. Kharas, R. Tatucu, M. Haddad, M. Brahmbhatt, R. Rajan, E.Vostroknutova, D. Bhattasali, G. Datt, S. Jayasuriya, T. Kong, E. Mountfield, and C. Ozer. 2007. *An East Asian Renaissance: Ideas for Economic Growth.* Washington, DC: World Bank.

Grey, S. 2001. "Women and Parliamentary Politics: Does Size Matter? Critical Mass and Women MPs in the New Zealand House of Representatives." Paper prepared for the 51st Political Studies Association Conference, Manchester, UK, April 10–12. http://www.capwip.org/readingroom/nz_wip.pdf.

Horn, Z. E. 2009. "No Cushion to Fall Back On: The Global Economic Crisis and Informal Workers." Online report for Women in Informal Employment: Globalizing and Organizing (WIEGO). http://www.inclusivecities.org/pdfs/GEC_Study.pdf.

HR Inc., and MCG Management Consulting. 2008. "Impact Assessment of the Public-Private Dialogue Initiatives in Cambodia, Lao PDR, Vietnam." International Finance Corporation, Washington, DC.

IFC (International Finance Corporation). 2006. "Voices of Women in the Private Sector (Indonesia)." Report for the IFC and the Mekong Private Sector Development Facility, IFC, Washington, DC. http://www.ifc.org/ifcext/sustainability.nsf/AttachmentsByTitle/p_Gender_IndonesiaVoices/$FILE/Indonesia+Voices_full_english.pdf.

ILO (International Labour Organization). 2009. "Technical Note Asia in the Global Economic Crisis: Impacts and Responses from a Gender Perspective." ILO, Bangkok.

Klapper, L., L. Laeven, and R. Rajan. 2006. "Entry Regulation as a Barrier to Entrepreneurship." *Journal of Financial Economics* 82 (3): 591–629.

Malesky, Edmund J., Doan Ngoc Minh, Nguyen Thanh Hai, Vu Thanh Tu Anh, Dau Anh Tuan, Duong Duc Lan, and Dau Anh Tuan. 2008. "Provincial Economic Governance and Its Impact on Local Competitiveness." *Business Issues Bulletin* 23 (26): 1. http://www.ifc.org/ifcext/mekongpsdf.nsf/AttachmentsByTitle/BIB-26-Vn-Eng/$FILE/BIB-26-Vn-Eng.pdf.

Nguyen, Thai Dung; Dinh Duong Nguyen, Phuong Bac Nguyen, John Schjelderup Olaisen; Quang Thinh Vu, Anh Tuan Nguyen, Thi Tuan Nguyen, Kim Quy Vu, and Van Hai Dang. 2006. "Starting a Business in Vietnam: How Easy." Briefing Paper, World Bank, Washington, DC.

UNESCAP (United Nations Economic and Social Commission for Asia and the Pacific). 2009. "Economic and Social Survey of Asia and the Pacific 2009: Addressing Triple Threats to Development." UNESCAP, Bangkok.

World Bank. 2003. *Doing Business in 2004.* Washington, DC: World Bank.

———. 2004. *Doing Business in 2005*. Washington, DC: World Bank.

———. 2005. *Doing Business in 2006*. Washington, DC: World Bank.

———. 2006a. *Doing Business in 2007*. Washington, DC: World Bank.

———. 2006b. "Indonesia: Country Gender Assessment." World Bank, Washington, DC.

———. 2007a. *Doing Business 2008*. Washington, DC: World Bank.

———. 2007b. "Informal Charges Hinder Business Growth in Cambodia." Briefing Paper 39812, World Bank, Washington, DC.

———. 2007c. "Lao—Private Sector and Investment Climate Assessment: Reducing Investment Climate Constraints to Higher Growth." Investment Climate Assessment, World Bank, Washington, DC.

———. 2007d. "Mongolia—Promoting Investment and Job Creation: An Investment Climate Assessment and Trade Integration Study." Investment Climate Assessment, World Bank, Washington, DC.

———. 2007e. "Philippines—Country Assistance Strategy Progress Report." CAS Progress Report, World Bank, Washington, DC.

———. 2007f. "Revitalizing the Rural Economy: An Assessment of the Investment Climate Faced by Non-Farm Enterprises at the District Level." Working Paper 38777, World Bank, Washington, DC.

———. 2008. *Doing Business 2009*. Washington, DC: World Bank.

———. 2009. *Doing Business 2010*. Washington, DC: World Bank.

———. 2010. *"Economic Opportunities for Women in East Asia and the Pacific."* Washington, DC: World Bank.

# CHAPTER 4

# Going for Growth

The discussion so far has focused, through a gender lens, on the basics of the entrepreneurial decision: the access to assets, the exercise of entrepreneurial agency to start up production, the negotiation of legal and regulatory constraints, and the management of general business environment issues.

Real-world entrepreneurship is, of course, far more complex. Once entrepreneurs have successfully obtained assets and navigated entry procedures to register as legal enterprises, they sometimes "go for growth." This often means gaining access to wider national and international markets for both inputs and products—especially in the export-oriented economies in the East Asia and Pacific region. Conversely, wherever the business environment is unfavorable or access to assets insecure, women entrepreneurs may get trapped in a vicious cycle of informality, enterprise failure, and continued impediments to negotiating regulatory requirements.

Many factors shape the obstacles and opportunities affecting successful enterprise growth. These factors include the trade regimes (including the number and cost of legal procedures); the domestic infrastructure (transport, communications, and power) that influences the costs and conditions of producing in large quantities and getting to market; and the information that entrepreneurs can obtain about consumer preferences and demand. Business development training and business extension services, particularly for small and medium-size enterprises (SMEs), can also play crucial roles. Intermediary organizations may catalyze business start-ups and growth. Finally, and obviously, women must continue to access assets—credit, labor, and their own time—to be able to scale up their businesses.

This section discusses the specific factors that can either help or hinder women in entering the *virtuous* cycle of business start-up, ease of access to markets, and incremental enterprise growth. These include: trade regulations, SME training and business development services, and the role of intermediary organizations.

## Trading across Borders

Several countries in the region have reaped large growth dividends through an export-oriented, labor-intensive growth model, often relying on a large pool of cheap female labor. Although export-led growth has undoubtedly increased women's economic opportunity and participation in several countries in developing East Asia (notably the Mekong region and Indonesia), women in the export-oriented sector have also experienced a marked disparity in their wages and quality of work and job security relative to men.

Comparing the changes in the real manufacturing wage index for women with the change in the wage gap (measured as a percentage of the male wage in manufacturing) shows that while, in absolute terms, real wages have risen for women in manufacturing over the past two decades, the gender gap in wages has been much slower to close. In some cases, such as in Hong Kong, China, the gap has actually widened during the boom years (see figure 4.1 for trends in selected "tiger" economies; note how much steeper the increase is in the real manufacturing wage index compared with the much flatter change in the female-male wage ratio figures).

Seguino (2000) has argued that, in developing East Asia, income equality at the household level is accompanied by *in*equality on gender lines at the individual level. This stimulates growth through two channels: (1) a positive effect on exports by offering a large pool of relatively cheap female labor for labor-intensive manufacturing, and (2) positive effects on investment through capital chasing higher marginal returns made possible through the relatively lower bargaining power of workers.

**Figure 4.1 Manufacturing Wage Trends for Women, Selected East Asian and Pacific Economies, 1983–2007**

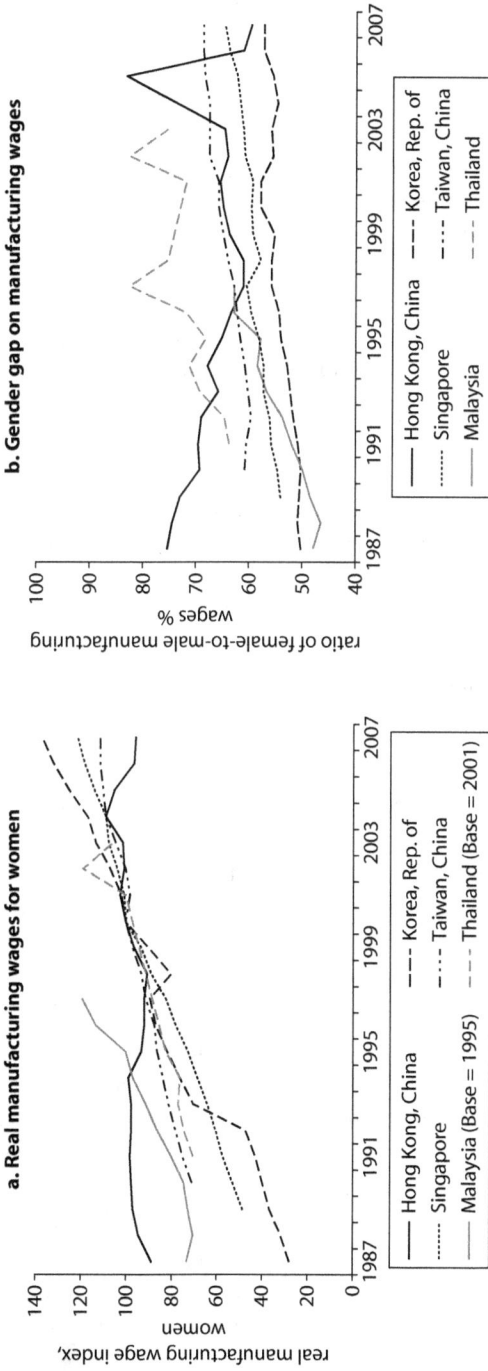

**a. Real manufacturing wages for women**

Legend:
— Hong Kong, China
······ Singapore
— Malaysia (Base = 1995)
--- Korea, Rep. of
···· Taiwan, China
--- Thailand (Base = 2001)

y-axis: real manufacturing wage index, women (0, 20, 40, 60, 80, 100, 120, 140)
x-axis: 1987, 1991, 1995, 1999, 2003, 2007

**b. Gender gap on manufacturing wages**

Legend:
— Hong Kong, China
······ Singapore
— Malaysia
--- Korea, Rep. of
···· Taiwan, China
--- Thailand

y-axis: ratio of female-to-male manufacturing wages % (40, 50, 60, 70, 80, 90, 100)
x-axis: 1987, 1991, 1995, 1999, 2003, 2007

*Source:* International Labour Organization Key Indicators of the Labour Market, 2007.

*Note:* The Real Manufacturing Wage Index (RWI) shows the average real manufacturing wage across occupations in a given country, disaggregated by sex in this case. By comparison to the base year, it provides a useful measure of changes in relative economic welfare for women over different time periods, by providing a proxy for income levels. Following the ILO, we first calculated a nominal wage index (NW$_i$) for year $i$ as a percentage of the value for the base year (2000) as follows:

$$NW_i = (W_i/W_0) * 100$$

where $W_0$ is the nominal wage for 2000 and $W_i$ the nominal wage for year $i$.

The RWI is then computed by dividing, for each year $i$, the nominal wage index (NW$_i$) by the corresponding Consumer Price Index (CPI) (P$_i$):

$$RW_i = (NW_i/P_i) * 100$$

All data are unadjusted for seasonal variations. The information often includes end-of-year bonuses and other special premiums. Occasionally, payments in kind are also included. Most establishment surveys are limited to registered establishments in the formal sector and exclude small enterprises. They do not include casual workers, contributing family members or the informal sector.

Several gendered characteristics of the export-led growth story of many of the region's economies are notable:

- Women have formed an increasing share of the paid labor force since the adoption of export-oriented strategies.
- Women's share of manufacturing jobs has risen and is higher than their share of jobs in the economy as a whole. Further, within the manufacturing sector, women have been concentrated in labor-intensive industries that produce primarily for export. The International Labour Organization (ILO) has estimated, for example, that women make up as much as 70–80 percent of the more than 27 million employees in export processing zones (EPZs) around the world (ILO 1998). While data disaggregated by region are not currently available, given the concentration of EPZs in East Asia, this finding is of particular significance to the region.
- Women employed in the manufacturing sector receive significantly lower wages than men, although the degree of gender wage inequality varies greatly within the region. Educational attainment, itself a reflection of gender inequality, explains some of this variation, but the gap remains large after controlling for productivity differentials (Seguino 2000). See box 4.1 for a more detailed presentation of country-level evidence on the gender-trade-growth nexus.

For female entrepreneurs and workers, international trade presents significant enhanced economic opportunity for *participation*. How well the increases in participation correlate with increases in economic welfare is more of an open question. Nonetheless, easier trade and better access to international markets do increase economic opportunities for entrepreneurs and workers alike. From this point of view, an environment that facilitates international trade is important.

However, the ease of trading across borders is uneven across the region. Several entrepreneurs profiled in this volume claim that the number and complexity of border procedures (as well as export and import costs) constrain their ability to scale up. Figure 4.2 compares the performance of economies in the region on the time needed to clear exporting procedures and the per-container cost to send goods out to international markets. Performance on both metrics vary enormously—from global–best-practice Singapore to countries such as Lao PDR and Mongolia, where both the time and the costs required for exporting are usuriously high. In Mongolia, both the length and unpredictability of procedures are serious trade issues (World Bank 2007).

**Box 4.1**

# Country-Level Evidence on the Impact of Gender on International Trade

Opening up to international trade can be a lever for reducing poverty, expanding job opportunities for both women and men, and spurring technology transfer, investment, and ultimately economic growth. However, integration with international markets has differential impacts on the owners of capital and labor, on the one hand, and on workers at different levels of the skills hierarchy on the other. Research at the country level suggests that although international trade can be a positive force for the expansion of women's participation in the labor market, it can also exacerbate economic inequality between women and men because women tend to be concentrated at the lower end of the skill ladder.

Country gender assessments for Cambodia, Lao PDR, the Philippines, and Vietnam all point to the role of export expansion in increasing women's participation in paid work, particularly in the labor-intensive manufacturing sector (ADB 2004; ADB 2002; ADB and World Bank 2008). However, several issues remain notable.

*Women are concentrated in certain sectors of these countries' export markets.* In the Philippines, for example, women constitute 63 percent of the electronics industry, concentrated in low-value-added and labor-intensive work. Whereas women constitute 85 percent of lower-paid production operators in that industry, the higher-paid technicians and engineers are almost always male (ADB and World Bank 2008). In Cambodia, the rapid rise in women's economic participation has been driven by the exporting garment industry. Rising participation has, in turn, contributed significantly to national growth. Women constitute 90 percent of the workforce in this industry, with garments contributing 94 percent of recent manufacturing growth (ADB 2004). In Lao PDR, women are concentrated in textiles as well as in commercial weaving and embroidery activities, and the country has established relationships with buyers in Thailand and overseas markets. However, the phaseout of quotas under the new World Trade Organization (WTO) regime has made the position of women garment workers across the region precarious as competition from lower-cost producers forces wages and labor standards down.

*Both women and men are vulnerable because of lax labor protections in export processing zones (EPZs).* In the Philippines, for example, EPZ workers are not allowed to join unions, and minimum contractual conditions (for example, paid leave) tend to be lower than national norms. Similar provisions apply in the EPZs in Cambodia.

*(continued)*

**Box 4.1** *(continued)*

*An economy-wide wage gap between men and women persists in these countries, particularly within the export sector.* This gap exists not only because women's wages are often lower but also because women engage in more irregular or contract work, which pays less.

This country-level evidence allows for some tentative observations, pending further poverty and social-impact analysis of international trade expansion. Although women's increased participation in international trade has expanded participation and employment in absolute terms, it has had ambiguous effects on gender equality in the labor market because

- Women, concentrated in low-value-added, low-skilled manufacturing work, lack the bargaining power against highly mobile capital to exact higher wages (Seguino 2000).
- Contract and temporary employment has grown in the export sector, reducing the social and other labor protections available in full-time contractual employment (ILO 2009).
- Countries have not invested enough in upgrading the skills of their female workforce, thus perpetuating their segmentation at the bottom of the value chain.

*Sources:* ADB 2002, 2004; ADB and World Bank 2008.

**Figure 4.2    Export Procedures and Costs, Selected East Asian and Pacific Economies**

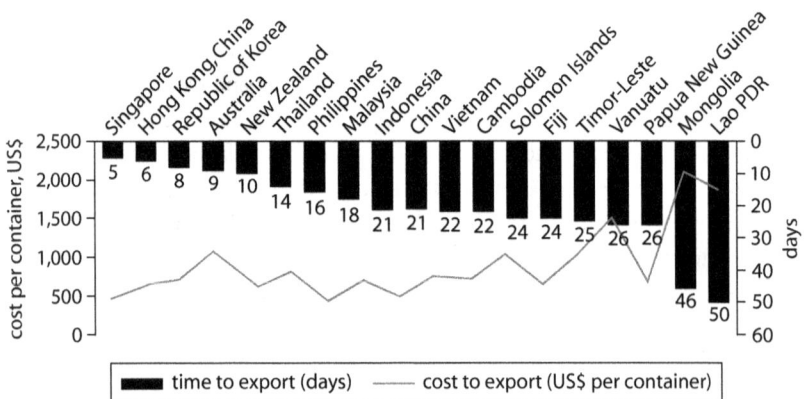

The number and complexity of customs procedures can also add quickly to scale-up costs and sometimes impose a binding constraint to accessing international markets or to meeting the scale and complexity of international orders. Research suggests that more efficient processes, along with increased transparency to reduce the opportunities for corruption, could significantly reduce trade costs in the region (Abe and Wilson 2008).

Although importing and exporting costs and tariff levels are generally low for the Association of Southeast Asian Nations (ASEAN) countries, the average number of documents and days required is well above the Organisation for Economic Co-operation and Development (OECD) average. It takes an average of 12 days and 6 documents to import into OECD countries. The average across ASEAN countries is 32 days and 11 documents (Shepherd and Wilson 2008).

Country-level research and case studies of individual female entrepre-neurs in the region confirm the serious burden that customs procedures impose, particularly on small export-oriented businesses. For example, in Cambodia, the lack of standardized procedures for air freight (used by the handicraft industry) as well as the number and costs of export procedures are cited as key constraints in a case study of a female entrepreneur (see box 4.2) (World Bank 2010). Similar concerns are raised in a case study of

**Box 4.2**

## Case Study Excerpt

### Cambodia: Sokorn Chom and Sotheary San
Members, Cambodian Craft Cooperation (CCC)

Historically, silk has held a significant place in Cambodian life and culture; in the 7th century, Cambodia was a busy trading stop on the famous Silk Road linking China to Europe.

Sokorn Chom and Sotheary San come from an area of Cambodia renowned for its silk weavers. In the past, they used to supplement their farming incomes by weaving during the dry season. However, seasonal price fluctuations and the strong bargaining power of middlemen meant that their ability to generate income was limited and unpredictable.

In 1997, Sotheary and Sokorn were able to gain power in numbers by joining the Cambodian Craft Cooperation (CCC), a Khmer nongovernmental organization (NGO). With the assistance of the International Trade Centre, the CCC has enabled

*(continued)*

**Box 4.2** *(continued)*

its members to stabilize prices and compete in international markets by establishing fixed product prices and profit margins; surveying European markets and presenting CCC's products to potential buyers during trade fairs; introducing women to more efficient modern handweaving looms; teaching women to use AZO-free environmental and health friendly dyes in order to meet export standards; and encouraging weavers to develop contemporary designs that would be more attractive to European customers. Although the CCC has succeeded in helping members access international markets and raise their monthly incomes from an average of US$40 to US$200, the high costs associated with exporting from Cambodia continue to damage the competitiveness of its members' products.

In the *Doing Business 2010* report, Cambodia ranks 127 out of 183 economies for the ease of trading across borders. An average of 22 days and 11 documents are required to export goods. The problem is made even more acute for Sotheary and Sokorn because they must ship their goods by air; the high value, low quantity, and time sensitivity of their shipments to Europe makes air shipping the obvious choice. However, the Ministry of Commerce has not developed standardized administrative procedures for air freight as it has done for export by sea. This means that air freight is subject to extra delays and makes it necessary for exporters to pay an extra fee of up to US$200 if they want to expedite the process. Because orders from international clients can be quite time sensitive, most exporters reportedly choose to pay this extra fee.

*Sources:* World Bank 2009, 2010.

a female entrepreneur in Fiji. The owners of Pure Fiji, a manufacturer of beauty care products, echo other small businesses in Fiji in their concerns over the costs associated with customs regulations (World Bank 2010).

SMEs, often producing specialized goods catering primarily to international markets, are particularly affected by cumbersome border procedures. In a survey of SMEs in Fiji, Papua New Guinea, Samoa, Tonga, and Vanuatu, the highest number of firms rated customs regulations as the most serious regulatory barrier for business (IFC 2003).

The role of corruption was discussed at length in chapter 3 as a general business environment issue. Research suggests that, in some countries, trade procedure and administrators are particularly affected by corruption (Abe and Wilson 2008). Data from other regions suggest that women entrepreneurs are especially affected by corruption; in Uganda, for example, 43 percent of female-headed businesses reported interference by government officials, compared to just 25 percent of male-headed businesses (Ellis, Manuel, and Blackden 2006).

A greater role for e-government processes could help reduce opportunities for corruption and expedite customs procedures, thus allowing businesses to lower the costs of trade. Evidence from Ghana showed decreases in bribery and increases in customs revenues as a result of the government's GhanaNet online customs facilitation (ITC, UNCTAD, and WTO 2007). Encouragingly, some countries in the East Asia and Pacific region—Thailand, for example—have started to implement such online systems.

The ability to safely and quickly move themselves and their products to ports of exit or marketplaces is another specific concern for women. If a household has access to a vehicle, it is usually the husband or man of the house who has control over it, while women must rely on often-inefficient public transportation. This can also pose a security concern for women traveling alone (ITC, UNCTAD, and WTO 2007).

## The Role of Intermediary Institutions

Intermediary organizations are often crucial to the "going for growth" process of microenterprises. They may be especially critical for women, who often operate microenterprises or informal businesses and do not have the same access as men to trade support networks (Domeisen 2004). Cross-national research indicates that forming groups and associations would be useful to accomplish the following:

- Get discounts on fees demanded by the authorities.
- End isolation of individual clientele, and increase access to markets by bypassing middlemen.
- Engage in risk pooling and risk sharing, as appropriate, to access credit on better terms.
- Reap economies of scale in production and through the bulk buying of inputs.

Research, especially cross-national data, on patterns of access to intermediary organizations and potential for collective organization is hard to come by in this region. However, qualitative and anecdotal research hints at the positive role intermediary institutions have played in catalyzing women's business. A report prepared for Asia-Pacific Economic Cooperation (APEC) discusses intermediary institutions as "crucial" enablers of women-led, export-oriented enterprise in Indonesia, the Republic of Korea, Thailand, and Vietnam because they reduce otherwise unaffordable transaction costs and help women-led enterprises to organize to supply international markets (Gibb 2004). Similarly, studies of microvendors in Cambodia and of women entrepreneurs in general in Vietnam cite the positive roles that intermediary institutions have played in the scale-up process of women-led enterprises (Agnello and Moller 2006; VWEC 2007).

A case study of a female entrepreneur in Cambodia highlights the role of the Cambodian Craft Cooperation (CCC) in generating an international market for its members' products. The CCC has also helped members to navigate complex trade and customs clearance obstacles. Similarly, the Export-led Poverty Reduction Program (EPRP) of the International Trade Centre (ITC) supported export market development on behalf of cottage industry (World Bank 2010).

The ITC's Women and Trade Program operates in other countries of the region as well as internationally, offering support to governments to engender their trade strategies; encouraging trade support institutions to offer outreach to women entrepreneurs; and helping women entrepreneurs to develop the skills necessary to compete in international markets (see box 4.3). Another option for women entrepreneurs is to form clusters of producers to benefit from economies of scale and be better able to satisfy large orders; an example is the collaborative effort by 500 artisans in India in the production of shoes (ITC, UNCTAD, and WTO 2007).

Although there are clearly positive steps in the direction of integrating small women-led enterprises with international markets, the scope and coverage of trade outreach by these organizations is still limited. For example, the ADB country gender assessment for Cambodia notes that women's cottage firms remain largely "invisible"—cut off from market information, credit, and regulation (ADB 2004).

## Business Development Services and Training

The provision of targeted training for SMEs can be a crucial part of a government's private sector development strategy. OECD research found "a positive correlation between the degree of management training and the bottom-line performance of an SME" (SPRING Singapore 2008). The growth of such training programs especially benefits women, who might lack other avenues to business development

**Box 4.3**

# Connecting Women with International Markets: The International Trade Centre

Few trade policies sufficiently consider gender issues. This is a glaring omission if trade policy is meant to contribute to poverty reduction, as 70 percent of the world's poor are women. The ITC's Women and Trade program is working to assist trade support institutions and governments to ensure that trade strategies take gender issues into account and to help strengthen these organizations' links to women entrepreneurs. The program has three main objectives:

- Improving policy makers' capacity to design, implement, and evaluate export strategies and national development plans that build on the role of women in trade
- Improving the representation of women and gender issues in trade support institutions
- Improving the competitiveness of women-owned enterprises in developing countries

ITC's work with the Cambodian government presents a good example of its work with developing countries in East Asia. Cambodia included the impact of international trade on female employment in its 2007 Diagnostic Trade Integration Study (DTIS). Silk weaving and the production of silk products were identified as having a medium-to-high human development impact, with particular importance for women. The ITC then worked with the Cambodian government to develop a silk sector strategy. The subsequent investment in the export potential of the silk sector helped to reduce rural poverty generally and to increase the economic empowerment of women more specifically.

The DTIS helped to facilitate south-south learning from such examples of good practice through its support to the Expert Round Table on the Gender Dimension of the Enhanced Integrated Framework in 2008. The meeting brought together developing countries, the WTO, and numerous experts to discuss how to better address gender issues in the Enhanced Integrated Framework—a mechanism through which trade-related aid is channeled. The meeting resulted in a document outlining 24 case studies of best practices and lessons learned on the subject of "unlocking women's trade potential."

*Source:* International Trade Centre.

services, training, market information, and market niches they might fill. Women in developing countries are already active in providing products and services for the local market but often lack the scale, quality, and efficiency to expand their businesses and to trade internationally (ITC, UNCTAD, and WTO 2007).

Training is not enough, however. SME training and business development services must be geographically accessible to both men and women and affordable for intended beneficiaries. Moreover, the length and quality of training must take into account the other time burdens that female entrepreneurs face if such training is to truly catalyze the SME sector. Working women, particularly working mothers, need training programs that are suitably timed and do not take them away from their families for an extended period of time. The consideration of women's needs when setting training schedules was one of the reasons that the "ACCESS!" export training programs in Ethiopia were so successful (ITC, UNCTAD, and WTO 2007). The EIU's qualitative assessment of the availability of SME training takes the abovementioned criteria into account. Figure 4.3

**Figure 4.3    Quality of SME Training and Business Development, Selected East Asian and Pacific Economies**

*EIU 5-point scale*

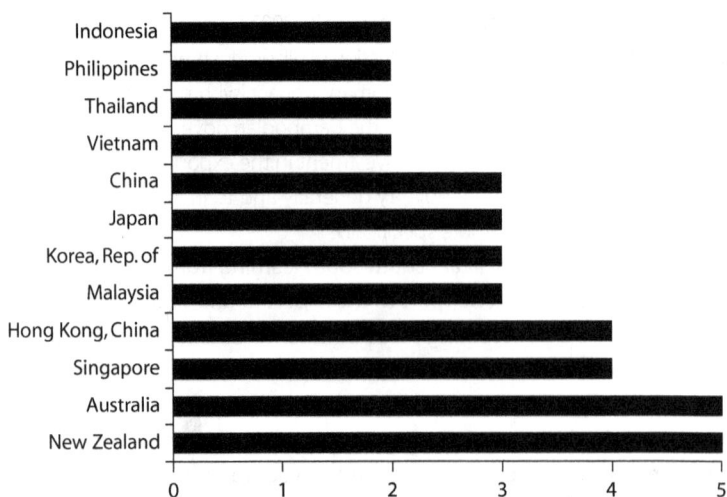

Source: EIU, forthcoming.
Note: EIU, Economist Intelligence Unit. An EIU qualitative analysis calculated the score on a 5-point scale that assesses the following five criteria for high-quality training programs: (1) wide geographic availability, (2) accessibility to both women and men, (3) affordability, (4) cultural appropriateness, and (5) consideration of women's time burdens in setting the length of training.

presents the scores, where available, for East Asia and Pacific region countries on this indicator.

The scores consider the following five conditions: training programs have wide geographic availability, are accessible to women as well as men, are affordable for most of the intended beneficiaries, are culturally appropriate, and take into account women's time burdens for the length of training. Countries score 1.0 if they meet one or none of the conditions, they score 2.0 if they meet at least two conditions, and so forth. The quality of SME support and training varies from a low of 2.0 in countries such as Indonesia, Thailand, and Vietnam to a high of 5.0 for Australia and New Zealand. Clearly, efforts can be greater in many of the region's economies to support women-led businesses and provide targeted SME training.

Globally, training courses for the export of services do not seem to be reaching women; while 75 percent of businesses in the service sector are owned by women, women make up only 4 percent of participants in training courses for businesses in the sector (ITC, UNCTAD, and WTO 2007). Business development services in general are also unevenly available and accessed by women entrepreneurs in the Asia Pacific region. Country-level work (for example, in Vietnam) reveals constraints on both the supply and demand sides (VWEC 2007).

Service providers lack a clear understanding of the specific needs of local businesses, particularly those led by women. Business development service firms in the region lack consulting skills and experience; in particular, they cannot articulate effectively the value of consulting services to clients. On the demand side, a lack of awareness and resources limits effective demand for business development providers. Both deficits must be addressed—strengthening provider supply and stimulating client demand—to promote the graduation from microenterprises to larger, self-sustaining enterprises.

## Opportunities to Learn and Reform: Going to Scale

Unleashing and enabling women entrepreneurs to "go for growth" and move from small-scale, largely household-based production to larger, viable, commercialized enterprises require a number of steps.

- *Trading across borders must become easier* in terms of complexity, number, and costs of procedures. Governments have more control over some of these variables than others; while international shipping costs may be largely outside their control, governments can greatly simplify import requirements so that women can get, at fair-duty rates, the most competitively priced inputs for their products. Moreover, easing export procedures (through e-government services and one-stop export clearance requirements) would undoubtedly boost women's ability to trade in larger international markets. Thailand provides a notable success story in this area, as a case study of a Thai female entrepreneur attests (World Bank 2010).

- *Franchising models should be explored* as a means of extending enterprises and helping start-ups to more easily navigate credit and procedural requirements.
- *Tailored business development services must become more widely available*, taking into account the particular needs of women entrepreneurs in different market segments and at different stages of enterprise sophistication. Support for SMEs through business development services and targeted training may well help catalyze the virtuous cycle.
- *Intermediary organizations should be strengthened*, particularly those that cater to women and foster mutually beneficial forms of collective action in terms of negotiating regulations, obtaining assets, and achieving economies of scale in national and international markets. In this context, cooperative models for cottage (handicraft) and textile industries might hold great potential. Specifically, such organizations can help women negotiate better access to credit, combine their productive capacity to supply international markets, and receive comprehensive business development activities, filling a crucial gap (Gibb 2004).

## References

Abe, Kazutomo, and John S. Wilson. 2008. "Governance, Corruption, and Trade in the Asia Pacific Region." Policy Research Working Paper WPS4731, World Bank, Washington, DC. http://www-wds.worldbank.org/servlet/WDSContentServer/WDSP/IB/2008/09/29/000158349_20080929091251/Rendered/PDF/WPS4731.pdf.

ADB (Asian Development Bank). 2002. "Women in Vietnam: Country Briefing Paper." ADB, Manila. http://www.adb.org/Documents/Books/Country_Briefing_Papers/Women_in_VietNam/women_vie.pdf.

———. 2004. "Country Gender Assessment: Cambodia." ADB, Manila. http://www.adb.org/Documents/Reports/Country-Gender-Assessments/cga-cam.pdf.

ADB (Asian Development Bank) and World Bank. 2008. "Joint Country Gender Assessment: Philippines." ADB, Manila. http://www.adb.org/Documents/Reports/Country-Gender-Assessments/phi-2008.asp.

Agnello, F., and J. Moller. 2006. "Vendors' Livelihoods: Women Micro-Entrepreneurs and Their Business Needs, Phnom Penh, Cambodia." ISED (Institute for Social and Economic Development) Series, ILO (International Labor Organization), Geneva. http://www.ilo.org/wcmsp5/groups/public/---asia/---robangkok/documents/publication/wcms_103492.pdf.

Domeisen, N. 2004. "Focus on Women Exporters." *International Trade Forum* (International Trade Centre) 40 (2): 35. http://www.tradeforum.org/news/fullstory.php/aid/667/Focus_on_Women_Exporters.html.

EIU (Economist Intelligence Unit). Forthcoming.

Ellis, A., C. Manuel, and M. Blackden. 2006. *Gender and Economic Growth in Uganda: Unleashing the Power of Women.* Directions in Development Series. Washington, DC: World Bank.

Gibb, H. 2004. "Supporting Potential Women Exporters." Report for the Asia-Pacific Economic Cooperation (APEC) Committee on Trade and Investment, APEC Secretariat and The North-South Institute, Ottawa. http://www.apec.org/apec/documents_reports/small_medium_enterprises_working_group/2004.MedialibDownload.v1.html?url=/etc/medialib/apec_media_library/downloads/workinggroups/smewg/mtg/2004/pdf.Par.0047.File.v1.1.

IFC (International Finance Corporation). 2003. "Pacific Enterprise Development Facility SME Business Survey." Powerpoint presentation delivered at IFC meetings in Fiji and Sydney, Australia.

ILO (International Labour Organization). 1998. "Export Processing Zones." *World of Work* 27 (December): 18–20. http://www.ilo.org/public/english/bureau/inf/magazine/ 27/news.htm.

————. 2009. "Technical Note Asia in the Global Economic Crisis: Impacts and Responses from a Gender Perspective." ILO, Bangkok.

ITC (International Trade Centre), UNCTAD (United Nations Conference on Trade and Development), and WTO (World Trade Association). 2007. *Innovations in Export Strategies: Gender Equality, Export Performance, and Competitiveness; The Gender Dimension of Export Strategy.* Geneva: ITC. http://www.intracen.org/wedf/ef2008/Montreux/PDFS/Gender-dimension-of-export-strategy.pdf.

Seguino, Stephanie. 2000. "Accounting for Asian Economic Growth." *Feminist Economics* 6 (3): 27–58.

Shepherd, Ben, and John S. Wilson. 2008. "Trade Facilitation in ASEAN Member Countries: Measuring Progress and Assessing Priorities." Policy Research Working Paper WPS4615, World Bank, Washington, DC.

SPRING Singapore (Standards, Productivity, and Innovation Board). 2008. "Growing BIG on Corporate Leadership." *Enterprise Today* (March/April) 2008.

VWEC (Vietnam Women Entrepreneurs Council). 2007. "Women's Entrepreneurship Development in Vietnam." Research report. International Labor Organization in Vietnam, Hanoi. http://www.ilo.org/wcmsp5/groups/public/---asia/---ro-bangkok/documents/publication/wcms_100456.pdf.

World Bank. 2007. "Mongolia—Promoting Investment and Job Creation: An Investment Climate Assessment and Trade Integration Study." Investment Climate Assessment, World Bank, Washington, DC.

———. 2009. *Doing Business 2010.* Washington, DC: World Bank.

———. 2010. "*Economic Opportunities for Women in East Asia and the Pacific Region.*" Washington, DC: World Bank.

# Index

Boxes, figures, notes, and tables are indicated by *b, f, n,* and *t* following page numbers.

## ECO-AUDIT
### *Environmental Benefits Statement*

The World Bank is committed to preserving endangered forests and natural resources. The Office of the Publisher has chosen to print *Economic Opportunities for Women in the East Asia and Pacific Region* on recycled paper with 50 percent post-consumer waste, in accordance with the recommended standards for paper usage set by the Green Press Initiative, a nonprofit program supporting publishers in using fiber that is not sourced from endangered forests. For more information, visit www.greenpressinitiative.org.

Saved:
- 5 trees
- 2 million BTU's of total energy
- 455 lbs of $CO_2$ equivalent of greenhouse gases
- 2,192 gallons of waste water
- 133 pounds of solid waste

green
press
INITIATIVE

www.ingramcontent.com/pod-product-compliance
Lightning Source LLC
Chambersburg PA
CBHW070927270326
41927CB00011B/2760